A NATURALIST'S GUIDE TO THE

REPTILES & AMPHIBIANS OF NEW ZEALAND

Samuel Purdie

JOHN BEAUFOY PUBLISHING

First published in the United Kingdom and New Zealand in 2022 by John Beaufoy Publishing Ltd
11 Blenheim Court, 316 Woodstock Road, Oxford OX2 7NS, England
www.johnbeaufoy.com

10 9 8 7 6 5 4 3 2 1

Photo Credits
Front cover: *main image* Jewelled Gecko; *bottom row, left to right* Southland Green Skink, Hochstetter's Frog, Awakōpaka Skink, all © Samuel Purdie. **Back cover:** Hura Te Ao Gecko © Samuel Purdie.
Title page: Otago Skink © Samuel Purdie
Contents page: Whitaker's Skink © Samuel Purdie

ISBN 978-1-913679-31-6

Edited by Krystyna Mayer
Designed by Nigel Partridge
Printed and bound in Malaysia by Times Offset (M) Sdn. Bhd.

·CONTENTS·

INTRODUCTION

Aotearoa/New Zealand is a temperate paradise that is home to some of the most extraordinary wildlife on the planet. The unique biogeography of this Cretaceous lifeboat has stimulated diversity and allowed its biota to retain ancient adaptations or develop remarkable new ones. Numerous endemic birds have become flightless and/or nocturnal, such as kiwi (*Apteryx* spp.), and the Takahē (*Porphyrio hochstetteri*) and Kākāpō (*Strigops habroptilus*). Others became gigantic, like the now-extinct moa (Dinornithiformes) and Haast's Eagle (*Aquila moorei*); some developed extreme intelligence, like the Kea (*Nestor notabilis*) and Kākā (*N. meridionalis*). However, despite what some people may think, biological complexity and diversity are not limited to Aotearoa's/New Zealand's marvellous, charismatic birds. In fact, among its most diverse vertebrates are the spectacular reptiles and amphibians.

Currently, 128 taxa comprise Aotearoa's/New Zealand's endemic herpetofauna. This includes one species of Tuatara (*Sphenodon punctatus*), 49 species of gecko, 76 species of skink and four species of frog. Additionally, there are four species of native marine snake, and five species of marine turtle that are considered non-residential. There is also one species of exotic skink that has become naturalized, the Delicate (Rainbow) Skink (*Lampropholis delicata*). Aotearoa's/New Zealand's endemic terrestrial species are nestled within four families. All seven endemic gecko genera (*Tukutuku, Naultinus, Toropuku, Mokopirirakau, Dactylocnemis, Hoplodactylus* and *Woodworthia*) belong to the family Diplodactylidae, and the single skink genus (*Oligosoma*) belongs to the family Scincidae (subfamily Eugongylinae). These lizards probably dispersed to Aotearoa/New Zealand (possibly from Australia) over the last 50 million years following the separation of the Aotearoa/New Zealand subcontinent from the supercontinent Gondwana. However, endemic frogs and the Tuatara are thought to have vicariant origins and have existed in Aotearoa/New Zealand for more than 80 million years.

Aotearoa's/New Zealand's endemic *Leiopelma* frogs belong to the ancient family Leiopelmatidae, which probably emerged before the dinosaurs, between 170 and 210 million years ago (mya). Consequently, Aotearoa's/New Zealand's leiopelmatid frogs are among the most archaic frogs on the planet. The final, and perhaps most notable, reptile family is Sphenodontidae, to which the tuatara belong. This family belongs to the order

Rhynchocephalia, a group of reptiles that evolved more than a quarter of a billion years ago. Sphenodontid reptiles were widespread as late as the Cretaceous Period (145–66 mya), but the Tuatara is the sole surviving representative and has remained relatively unchanged since then.

The recently discovered Hura Te Ao Gecko (Mokopirirakau galaxias) is perfectly adapted to an alpine existence.

*The semi-webbed toes of the ancient Hochstetter's Frog (*Leiopelma hochstetteri*).*

Accordingly, it is often referred to as a 'living fossil'. It is truly one of the most unique and prehistoric reptiles on the planet. Its ancestors rose from the detritus of a global cataclysm that wiped out the dinosaurs. However, the greatest threat these magnificent reptiles would face was the arrival of humans and the introduction of mammalian predators.

For more than 80 million years, Aotearoa's/New Zealand's endemic herpetofauna evolved in the absence of mammals (except several bat species). Their only major predators were birds. They were not equipped to withstand the introduction of mammalian predator. Cats, mustelids, rodents and hedgehogs have become highly problematic and severely impacted reptile and amphibian populations everywhere on mainland Aotearoa/New Zealand. Most of these predators are primarily nocturnal, which has been particularly problematic for larger, ground-dwelling nocturnal herpetofauna. Historically, reptiles like the Tuatara, Robust Skink (*Oligosoma alani*), McGregor's Skink (*O. mcgregori*), Whitaker's

*Jewelled gecko (*Naultinus gemmeus*) in tussockland destroyed by fire.*

Carey Knox

Skink (*O. whitakeri*) and Duvaucel's geckos (*Hoplodactylus* spp.) were widespread on the mainland. The arrival of mammalian predators led to their rapid extirpation, and they are now mostly restricted to predator-free offshore islands. Due to the large size of these lizards, their refugia are more accessible to predators. It is therefore not surprising that more than 30 per cent of Aotearoa's/New Zealand's reptile taxa are threatened with extinction, and another 50 per cent are at risk of extinction. Terrestrial frogs like Archey's Frog (*Leiopelma archeyi*) and Hamilton's Frog (*L. hamiltoni*) have also suffered immensely, and at least three frog species have become extinct: the Aurora Frog (*L. auroraensis*), Waitomo Frog (*L. waitomoensis*) and Markham's Frog (*L. markhami*).

The scourge of these predators is exacerbated by habitat modification. Following the arrival of humans, nearly three-quarters of native forest habitat has been destroyed. This has meant that species with specific habitat, climatic or dietary preferences have suffered immensely. Additionally, reptiles and amphibians in modified habitats are more likely to suffer from natural weather events. This is particularly true for skink species on the West Coast of the South Island, where much of the remaining habitat for lizards like the Kapitia Skink (*Oligosoma salmo*), Cobble Skink (*O.* aff. *infrapunctatum* 'Cobble') and Hokitika Skink (*O.* aff. *infrapunctatum* 'Hokitika') is structurally homogenous (for example, pasture), close to the encroaching ocean and often subjected to extreme weather.

The future for many of Aotearoa's/New Zealand's species is concerning when considering the frightening prospect of climate change. Extreme weather events are predicted to occur more frequently, wildfires will be more likely to ignite, and ectotherms in the alpine region

Cascade Gecko (Mokopirirakau 'Cascades') with brilliant dorsal colouration.

will become increasingly accessible to predators. Unfortunately, Aotearoa's/New Zealand's remarkable herpetofauna possesses a range of biological, ecological and behavioural characteristics that have exacerbated the suite of impacts they are faced with. Most species can be extremely long lived, and their maximum potential lifespans remain largely unknown. Skinks can exceed 50 years, geckos 50 years, frogs 40 years and the Tuatara 100 years. Accordingly, they often have extended periods of maturation, and give birth to few young. This has meant that following crises, many populations struggle to recover and invariably decline over time.

There has been a surge of research and conservation work focused on Aotearoa's/New Zealand's amazing reptiles and amphibians. Many organizations are actively restoring habitats and conducting predator control to assist the native herpetofauna. Due to large-scale ecological restoration projects like Mokomoko Dryland Sanctuary, Zealandia Te Māra a Tāne Ecosanctuary, Orokonui Ecosanctuary, Maungatautari Sanctuary Mountain, Tāwharanui Open Sanctuary, Mahakirau Forest Estate and countless other offshore island projects, the future for many species is secure for now. These endeavours, combined with education projects, will hopefully increase the awareness of how astounding Aotearoa's/Aotearoa's/New Zealand's reptiles and amphibians truly are.

GEOGRAPHY & CLIMATE

More than 300 million years ago, the Earth was dominated by a supercontinent called Pangaea. The southern half of Pangaea was called Gondwanaland, which eventually formed the modern continents of Africa, South America, Australia, Antarctica and Aotearoa/New Zealand. During the Jurassic Period (199–145 mya), convection currents in the Earth's mantle caused immense slabs of continental crust to drift apart. Then, 80 million years ago, the Aotearoa/New Zealand subcontinent, Te Riu-a-Māui/Zealandia, was separated from Gondwanaland and began to move southwards. It experienced a long history of tectonic affliction and marine inundation, but eventually arrived in the South Pacific, at a temperate latitude between 35° and 47° S.

Aotearoa/New Zealand now comprises three major islands: Te Ika-a-Māui/North Island, Te Waipounamu/South Island and Rakiura/Stewart Island. There are also numerous other islands surrounding Aotearoa/New Zealand. The country is situated on a plate boundary, which has induced a range of geological processes. In northeastern Aotearoa/New Zealand, the Pacific plate is actively experiencing subduction under the Indo-Australian plate. This has resulted in the recent uplift of multiple volcanoes, particularly on the Central Plateau and in the Auckland Region. Many of these volcanoes are still active or dormant, such as Mt Ruapehu, Mt Ngauruhoe, Mt Tongariro, Rangitoto, Mt Taranaki and Whakaari/White Island.

Volcanism has heavily modified lizard habitat over Aotearoa's/New Zealand's geological history. Rangitoto Island only erupted from the ocean within the last 1,000 years, yet is home to an array of reptiles such as the Moko Skink (*Oligosoma moco*), Raukawa Gecko (*Woodworthia maculata*) and Egg-laying Skink (*Oligosoma suteri*). The dispersal of pumice from Earth-rattling events like the Taupō eruption has also provided important habitat for lizards like Small-scaled Skinks (*O. microlepis*). However, in other areas, frequent volcanism and the destruction of forested habitats have rendered them unsuitable for many species. In southern Aotearoa/New Zealand, the Indo-Australian plate is actively experiencing subduction under the Pacific plate, which has resulted in extensive geologic movement. This is especially prominent in the South Island, along the Alpine Fault. Aotearoa's/New Zealand's highest peak, Aoraki/Mt Cook (3,724m), and the rest of Te Tiritiri o te Moana/Southern Alps are situated here. These summits began to rise within the last 20 million years, and the rate of uplift accelerated dramatically within the last three million years.

Geological and climatic activity also resulted in extended periods of glaciation, causing several reptile lineages to separate and speciate. Numerous species are now adapted to extreme high-elevation climates and precipitous terrain. Several species of forest gecko (*Mokopirirakau* spp.) exist in the alpine zone, with some occupying habitats more than 2,000m above sea level. The Barrier Skink (*Oligosoma judgei*) and Sinbad Skink (*O. pikitanga*) also exist at high elevations (≥1,000m), and occupy habitats pummelled by rocks, avalanches and severe weather. Several marine transgression events have also stimulated speciation events. One of the most notable examples is the formation of the Manawatu Strait during the Pliocene Epoch (5.4–2.4 mya), which probably drove many north–south splits of sister species like the Glossy Brown Skink (*O. zelandicum*) and Kakerakau Skink (*O. kakerakau*), Northern Duvaucel's Gecko (*Hoplodactylus duvaucelii*) and Southern Duvaucel's Gecko (*H. duvaucelii* 'Southern'), and Archey's Frog (*Leiopelma archeyi*) and Hamilton's Frog (*L. hamiltoni*).

These geological events, combined with the country's temperate latitude, have resulted in a magnificent landscape with a plethora of microclimates. Aotearoa/New Zealand has four distinct seasons, with mean annual temperatures of 10° C in southern regions and 16° C in northern regions. In southern Aotearoa/New Zealand, many reptiles become inactive during winter, and their habitat is often completely covered in snow. Accordingly, they have become behaviourally or physiologically specialized. Many nocturnal species thermoregulate by basking (usually in partial concealment) during the day. This means that, despite existing in a high-elevation climate, some species can achieve similar body temperatures to their lowland relatives and can even be active in temperatures below 1° C. Some lizards also have modified reproductive behaviour because of their high-elevation lifestyles. Cascade Geckos (*Mokopirirakau* 'Cascades') are known to have extended embryonic incubation periods of more than two years, and Harlequin Geckos (*Tukutuku rakiurae*) may even reproduce quadrennially. Reptiles and amphibians in northern Aotearoa/New Zealand are also less active during winter but are generally exposed to milder conditions and have longer activity windows than their hardy southern relatives.

HABITATS

Aotearoa/New Zealand is a complex land mass that boasts some of the most picturesque environments on Earth. Due to the country's dynamic geography and climate, you can travel from a subtropical coastal environment to an alpine snowfield in a matter of hours. The diversity and complexity of these habitats has significantly contributed to the uniqueness of the herpetofauna.

Coastal Many of Aotearoa's/New Zealand's species are coastal obligates and some occupy the ocean. The marine reptiles are predominantly migrant or vagrant, spending most of their time in pelagic environments, but they do occasionally grace the shorelines. Several species of native gecko and skink also occur on or near the shorelines. In fact, some even enter the ocean itself. The Shore Skink (*Oligosoma smithi*) and its relatives opportunistically feed around rock pools and will dive into water to evade threats. Similar behaviour even occurs in the rugged habitat of southwestern Aotearoa/New Zealand, where Fiordland Skinks (*O. acrinasum*) occasionally disperse between rocky islets in frigid, violent waves. These habitats have forced their inhabitants to develop specialized adaptions such as nasal glands for secreting salt.

Lowland Historically, native forest covered most of lowland Aotearoa/New Zealand – that is, terrestrial ecosystems below 500m. Stands of giant trees more than 40m tall used to dominate much of the North Island. However, these habitats have been extensively modified by humans and face their own suite of challenges, such as grazing from mammals and the plague of infectious diseases like myrtle rust and kauri dieback. Despite this, reptiles and amphibians persist in the lowlands, usually where intact vegetation is present. Many gecko species, such as the Pacific Gecko (*Dactylocnemis pacificus*) and Forest Gecko

Mature podocarp forest.

(*Mokopirirakau granulatus*), can be found in scrubby habitat near forest margins, or high off the ground in large trees. Striped skinks are also known to climb trees and have been found in epiphytic platforms tens of metres off the ground. The forest floor houses other species, such as the Copper Skink (*Oligosoma aeneum*), Ornate Skink (*O. ornatum*) and elusive Slight Skink (*O. levidensum*). However, these species tend to struggle without suitable ground cover or predator control. Conversely, there are several species that may indirectly benefit from the clearing of forests. Open-country species like grass skinks (*O. polychroma* clade) and McCann's Skink (*O. maccanni*) have expanded their range and possibly number in the millions. These species and others also occur in many people's gardens. However, they still suffer from habitat development and predation. Some lowland-dwelling species, such as the Southland Green Skink (*O. chloronoton*), also occupy wetland habitats. Unfortunately, more than 90 per cent of Aotearoa's/New Zealand's wetlands have been lost, and most of the remaining wetland habitats are heavily modified, encroached with weeds and unsuitable for the herpetofauna. Native frogs have also been severely impacted by habitat modification and have disappeared from most lowland areas in Aotearoa/New Zealand.

Montane and Subalpine Above the lowland environments are montane and subalpine areas, which extend from approximately 500 to 1,000m above sea level. These environments are more open and have markedly different vegetation. Large plateaux above 500m, like the Cascade Plateau and Denniston Plateau, often have a mix of herbaceous and woody plants, and typically host a variety of dense, prostrate vegetation like mānuka (*Leptospermum* spp.) or *Dracophyllum*. These plants are often important habitat for green

Montane schist tor systems – important habitat for Otago skinks and several other species.

geckos (*Naultinus* spp.), and several skink species have been seen climbing shrubs to feed and thermoregulate. Large creviced boulders and loose rocks often litter these areas, which makes them even more suitable for reptiles. However, higher elevations are typically exposed to more extreme weather and temperatures than the lowlands. Temperatures regularly drop below freezing, yet heliothermic reptiles, like Jewelled Geckos (*Naultinus gemmeus*), have been seen on snow-covered tussocks in icy conditions. In drier regions, such as inland Waitaha/Canterbury and the Te Manahuna/Mackenzie District, rocky stream beds also provide important habitat for lizards. Numerous threatened skink species occupy these areas, such as the Mackenzie Skink (*Oligosoma prasinum*), Long-toed Skink (*O. longipes*) and Scree Skink (*O. waimatense*). Unfortunately, montane stream beds are prone to flooding and some skink populations have declined dramatically following severe weather events. Wetlands and pākihi habitats also occur in these areas and host a variety of reptiles. In fact, the Critically Endangered Alborn Skink (*O. albornense*) is only known from a sliver of montane pākihi habitat on the West Coast of the South Island. Herbfield and tussockland also constitute important montane/subalpine habitat for a variety of skinks. Most of the green skink species (*O. chloronoton* complex) occupy montane or subalpine herbfield and tussockland, and can thrive in densely vegetated gully systems (when predator numbers are low). The montane and subalpine regions, particularly those of the South Island, boast a diverse assemblage of reptiles.

Alpine Alpine ecosystems occur above the natural tree line, but below permanent snow in the nival zone (1,000–2,200m). While reptiles are typically associated with warm, tropical

Tussockland and talus – prime habitat for numerous alpine lizard species.

Esteemed herpetologist Carey Knox moving across scree skink habitat.

environments, some of Aotearoa's/New Zealand's species have been forced to occupy formidable alpine habitats and are subjected to an extreme spectrum of climatic conditions. These areas are characterized by dramatic temperature fluctuations, high winds, low moisture and intense ultraviolet exposure. In the alpine zone of the western South Island (for example in Fiordland National Park), reptiles such as the elusive Awakōpaka Skink (*O. awakopaka*) are exposed to high rainfall, avalanches, rockfalls and extended periods of snow cover. They are forced to push the limits of reptile physiology to survive. Similarly, Black-eyed Geckos (*Mokopirirakau kahutarae*) have been found in the northern South Island inhabiting sheer rock bluffs at more than 2,000m. Plants in the alpine zone are generally dense and stout, so most of the available vegetation for reptiles comprises grasses or tussocks. To avoid lethal winter temperatures, lizards must seek shelter in burrows, deep crevices, scree or boulderfield. Climate change is yet another challenge these reptiles face. The impacts of climate change on Aotearoa/New Zealand's alpine reptiles are not fully understood, but it seems likely that mammalian predators will have increasing access to

Alpine rock tors in Westland. Only the hardiest lizards live in habitat at these elevations.

higher elevations. The alpine ecosystems are as imperilled as they are valuable, and it is essential that we protect them.

Reptile & Amphibian Identification

All native reptiles and amphibians are protected by the New Zealand Wildlife Act. However, if you have rescued a native reptile or amphibian from a pet cat or dog, please release it in some dense vegetation off the ground and in some branches (if it is a gecko) or on the ground near some rocks and logs (if it is a skink) near where it was found. If it is injured, or you are unsure, contact your local Department of Conservation office for advice. This field guide features several images of native reptiles being handled to showcase their size. Each of these animals is a legally obtained captive specimen and is being handled by professionals, who are permitted reptile keepers. When identifying herpetofauna, a variety of characteristics should be considered and observed. If possible, try and get a good look at the overall shape of the animal, and note whether it is large, small, robust or gracile. It is also important to note the shape of its head, size and length of its limbs, length of its toes, number of supraocular scales, size of its ear-hole and length of its tail (if this is intact). Beginner naturalists may struggle to understand some of these features, but after you have observed several species and individuals, these characteristics become more apparent. Additionally, the colours and patterns of animals can be immensely informative for identification. The most important features to note are the dorsal pattern, eye colour, mouth colour, body colour, colour and shape of stripes (for example smooth v rough), presence of speckles, spots or flecks, and belly colour. It is also very important to note the type of habitat and general location where you found a reptile. Disclosing the specific location is not advisable, as there is a risk that wildlife smugglers will exploit this information. Finally, it is always helpful to take photographs. When doing so, try to obtain an image of the animal's entire body, head and back. It is worthwhile zooming in on a lizard as close as possible and photographing it from several different angles.

Sexing herpetofauna can be very difficult, but it is possible for beginner naturalists to do so with some endemic species. Female geckos and skinks are easy to recognize when they are heavily gravid. Their lateral surfaces bulge outwards conspicuously, and they look very rotund. When they are not gravid, sexing is much more difficult. Female geckos generally have a flat vent compared to males, which bear a large hemipenal bulge (a sack containing their copulatory organs), which can be viewed from either side of the tail. This bulge is also typically flanked with large cloacal spurs that are used for mating. Females may bear cloacal spurs, but they are typically much smaller. Males are also typically longer and leaner than females, sometimes with proportionately larger heads. Skinks are much more difficult to sex and can only reliably be sexed if they have been captured. Male skinks generally have a vent that is very square in cross-section, often with a small dimple, whereas females tend to have a vent that is round in cross-section. Native frogs can only be sexed in the field based on size. Mature females can grow about 1cm larger than males, and in Hochstetter's Frogs, males typically have broader forelimbs than females. However, there is a considerable amount of overlap.

GECKO ANATOMY

Male Hura Te Ao Gecko (*Mokopirirakau galaxias*)

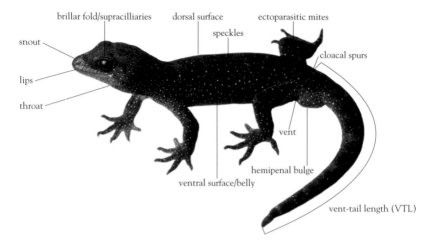

brillar fold/supracilliaries · dorsal surface · ectoparasitic mites · speckles · snout · lips · throat · cloacal spurs · vent · hemipenal bulge · ventral surface/belly · vent-tail length (VTL)

Female Ōkārito/Broad-cheeked Gecko (*Mokopirirakau* 'Ōkārito')

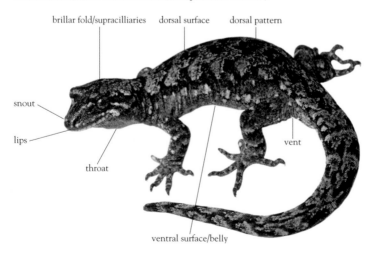

brillar fold/supracilliaries · dorsal surface · dorsal pattern · snout · lips · throat · vent · ventral surface/belly

■ REPTILE & AMPHIBIAN IDENTIFICATION ■

Forest Gecko (*Mokopirirakau granulatus*)
Head

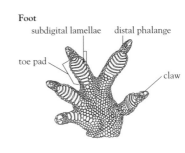

brillar fold/supraciliaries — eye
canthal scales
ear
nostril
rostral scale
infralabial scales
supralabial scales

Foot

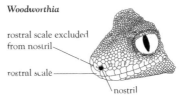

subdigital lamellae — distal phalange
toe pad
claw

Rostral scale comparison
Dactylocnemis

rostral scale in contact with nostril

rostral scale

nostril

Woodworthia

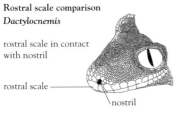

rostral scale excluded from nostril

rostral scale

nostril

SKINK ANATOMY
Barrier Skink (*Oligosoma judgei*)

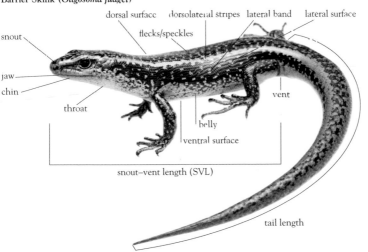

dorsal surface dorsolateral stripes lateral band lateral surface
flecks/speckles
snout
jaw
chin
throat
vent
belly
ventral surface
snout–vent length (SVL)
tail length

Big Bay Skink (*Oligosoma* aff. *inconspicuum* 'Big Bay')

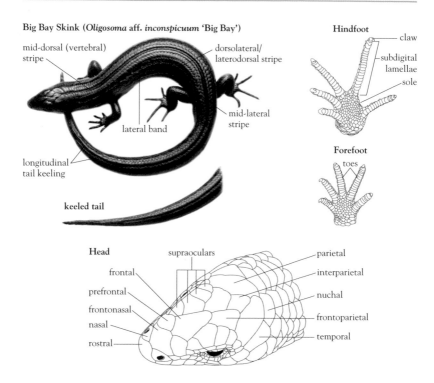

mid-dorsal (vertebral) stripe

dorsolateral/ laterodorsal stripe

lateral band

mid-lateral stripe

longitudinal tail keeling

keeled tail

Hindfoot

claw

subdigital lamellae

sole

Forefoot

toes

Head

supraoculars

frontal

prefrontal

frontonasal

nasal

rostral

parietal

interparietal

nuchal

frontoparietal

temporal

Lakes Skink (*Oligosoma* aff. *chloronoton* 'West Otago')

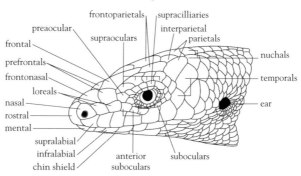

frontoparietals

supracilliaries

preaocular

supraoculars

interparietal

parietals

frontal

prefrontals

frontonasal

loreals

nasal

rostral

mental

nuchals

temporals

ear

supralabial

infralabial

chin shield

anterior suboculars

suboculars

FROG ANATOMY
Archey's Frog (*Leioplema archeyi*)

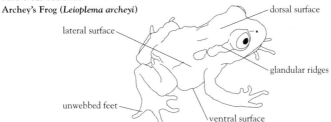

dorsal surface

lateral surface

glandular ridges

unwebbed feet

ventral surface

Southern Bell Frog (*Ranoidea raniformis*)

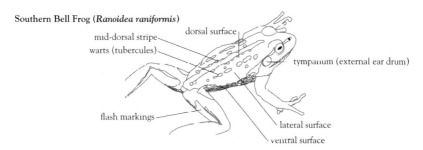

mid-dorsal stripe

warts (tubercules)

dorsal surface

tympanum (external ear drum)

flash markings

lateral surface

ventral surface

TURTLE ANATOMY
Green Turtle (*Chelonia mydas*)

prefrontal scales

claw

flipper

carapace/shell

vertebral scute

costal scute

ventral surface/plastron
(underneath)

SPECIES DESCRIPTIONS

Names Each species in this book is headed with a colloquial name. Some species have names that are confusing or uninformative, and in these cases alternatives are provided. The Northern Southern Alps Gecko is thus referred to as the Greywacke Gecko (due to its affinity to greywacke rock), the Southwestern Large Gecko as the Mountain Beech Gecko (due to its affinity to alpine areas and beech forest), the Northern Long-toed Skink as the Long-toed Skink (because the recently discovered Kahurangi Skink is the northernmost species in the Long-toed Skink clade), and the Plague (Rainbow) Skink as the Delicate (Rainbow) Skink (because the negative connotation of 'plague' may inadvertently lead to native skinks being killed).

Each species also has a scientific name that adheres to the binomial nomenclature system. The first part of the scientific name is referred to as the genus, the second part as the species. Because many of Aotearoa's/New Zealand's lizards are not formally described (due to a lack of taxonomic information), 'aff.' (affinity to a recognized clade/group), 'cf.' (compare), 'spp.' (species, plural), or 'sp.' (species, singular) may be used.

Measurements In most Aotearoa/New Zealand reptiles and amphibians, size is recorded using a standardized snout–vent length (SVL) measurement, which is taken from the tip of the snout to the cloacal vent on the ventral surface. The SVL measurements used in this book typically represent the largest known adults of each species. Accordingly, most reptiles or amphibians encountered are likely to be smaller than the size specified. Where species that resemble one another differ by size, and are directly compared in text, a more useful value is provided to illustrate the size ranges typically expected by adults (for example 'typically ≤70mm v ≥80mm SVL'). Straight carapace length (SCL), the measurement along the midline of the straight length of the carapace, is given for turtles. Total length (TL), measured from the snout-tip to the tail-tip, is given for snakes. The symbols ≤ (less than or equal to), ≥ (more than or equal to), < (less than) and > (more than) are also used to denote size.

Descriptions Morphology and colour descriptions are based on existing literature that has detailed the appearance of species (such as species description papers and existing field guides), personal observations (by the author and close colleagues), and photographic databases. Photographs used in scientific papers and field guides only capture a fraction of the variation seen in Aotearoa/New Zealand reptiles and amphibians, so photographic databases (like Carey Knox's Flickr page, Tony Jewell's Flickr page and the New Zealand Herpetological Society website; see p. 172) have been invaluable. Note that not every possible morphological variant for each species is mentioned. Conditions like melanism, hypomelanism, albinism, leucism and xanthochromism occur in a variety of species and result in atypical colour morphs. For example, Crenulate Skinks (*Oligosoma robinsoni*) are normally brown in colour, but aberrant black individuals have been found. Therefore, it is important to note not just the colour of a species when trying to identify it, but a variety of morphological features.

Xanthochromic Starred Gecko (Naultinus stellatus).

Xanthochromic Green and Golden Bell Frog (Ranoidea aurea).

Species Comparisons Many of Aotearoa's/New Zealand's reptiles look very similar and can only reliably be differentiated using genetic analyses or minute morphological features. Some are identifiable by their general 'look', although this is often difficult to describe. For example, an experienced herpetologist can quickly differentiate a Copper Skink from a Shore Skink by their dissimilar head shapes – but most people may think they look very similar. Thus, identifying lizards can sometimes be very difficult for beginner naturalists. Even the experts occasionally misidentify species. Many morphological features are poorly understood, variable, or somewhat subjective and occasionally fail. However, the author has endeavoured to use the most current and helpful information to discern species that closely resemble one another. Additionally, comparisons are mostly only drawn between species that are known to be (or may be) sympatric with one another (unless specified otherwise). This is to maximize the efficiency of identifying species in the field.

Distribution Each species description is accompanied by a distribution section and map. The distribution maps are simplified, with predicted distributions based on a combination of known distribution data, historical distribution data, suitability of habitat and known biogeographic patterns. Small island (or island group) populations or ecosanctuary populations (where current geographical range is not known to overlap) are represented by red triangles (with the exception of some islands in the Hauraki Gulf and Te Tauihu-o-te-Waka/Marlborough Sounds for display purposes). Larger islands (such as Aotea/Great Barrier, Hauturu/Little Barrier, Kāpiti Island) are coloured red.

Habits & Habitats Aotearoa/New Zealand herpetofauna occupy a range of habitats throughout Aotearoa/New Zealand. Here, their habitat preferences have been identified by utilizing similar information to that mentioned in the 'descriptions section'. Diet and reproductive behaviour for most species is not generally discussed, as this is similar for many of Aotearoa's/New Zealand's reptiles and amphibians. Most of Aotearoa's/New Zealand's herpetofauna opportunistically feed on a variety of invertebrates, berries, fruits, nectar sources and smaller conspecifics. All of Aotearoa's/New Zealand's endemic lizards are viviparous (except the Egg-laying Skink, *Oligosoma suteri*) and give birth to live young. Geckos typically produce two young, whereas skinks can produce up to eight. They mostly mate and reproduce annually or biennially during the warmer months in spring and summer. Tuatara lay up to 18 soft-shelled eggs, which remain buried for 16 months. The offspring of these eggs are largely determined by a physiological process called 'temperature-dependent sex determination'. In warmer conditions, offspring are male skewed, in cooler conditions female skewed. Endemic frogs (apart from Hochstetter's Frog, *Leiopelma hochstetteri*) do not have a free-swimming larval stage; instead, offspring emerge from eggs and climb on to their father's back, remaining there until they are capable of fending for themselves.

Conservation The current conservation status for each species is provided in the checklist (p. 168). This has been based on Hitchmough et al., 2021, 'Conservation status of New Zealand reptiles' (p. 172). The threats and conservation work conducted with species have also been discussed in the descriptions. However, threats and conservation programmes have not been described for all species in the book. Practically all Aotearoa/New Zealand reptiles and amphibians are impacted by mammalian predators and habitat modification, but this is only mentioned for species that are particularly impacted by these threats. The International Union for Conservation of Nature (IUCN) Red List threat status is given for marine species.

GLOSSARY

abundant Existing in high numbers or large quantities.

adaptation Trait or process of becoming better suited to an environment or niche.

albinism Congenital condition resulting in absence of pigments in parts of body including skin and eyes.

allopatric Relating to an organism that occupies a different or isolated geographical area from another organism.

alluvial fan Aggregation of sediments on a slope causing a large, fan-like land form.

anterior Relating to front of an organism or part of an organism.

arboreal Living in or climbing trees.

autotomy Casting off of part of body, like a lizard's tail, by an animal under threat. In lizards, the tail may regrow, but will not look the same as the original tail.

biennially Refers to process or event that takes place approximately once every two years.

binomial nomenclature Formal system used to classify organisms.

biogeography Geographical distribution of wildlife and its study.

biota Wildlife of an area.

boulderfield Habitat that is an aggregation of large rocks that are more than 256mm in diameter.

carapace Hardened upper shell, such as that in turtles.

cathemeral Active somewhat erratically during both night and day.

caudal Pertaining to tail.

cnidarian Group/phylum that jellyfish, sea anemones, hydras, corals and salps belong to.

convection currents Movement of materials caused by differential heating.

crepuscular Active mostly during dawn and dusk.

Cretaceous (Period) Period in geologic time between 145 and 66 million years ago.

cryptic Relates to shy, inconspicuous behaviour of an animal; difficult to find or observe.

Dinornithiformes Taxonomic group/order that moa belong to.

diurnal Active mostly during the day.

dorsal Relating to upper surfaces of an animal's body.

ecosanctuary Area that is either fenced off or has extensive trapping, rendering it free or almost free of mammalian predators.

ectotherm Organism that regulates its internal body temperature via external sources of heat/energy.

embryonic incubation Process of maintaining embryos at a suitable temperature so they can develop into offspring.

endemic Native and restricted to a certain area.

extirpation Elimination/extinction of an organism from an area.

flecks Markings that are usually fine or angular.

gravid Refers to pregnant animal.

heliothermic Relates to organisms that bask in direct sunlight to thermoregulate.

herbaceous Relates to vascular plants lacking woody stems.

herbfield Habitat comprising predominantly non-woody herbaceous plants like grasses, forbs and tussocks.

homogenous Comprising elements that are similar.

Jurassic (Period) Period in geologic time between 201 and 145 million years ago.

lateral Relating to surfaces on sides of an animal's body.

leucism Condition resulting in partial loss of pigments in parts of body (usually excluding eyes).

litter Detritus of fallen leaves, branches and bark that accumulates on forest floor.

longitudinal Relating to something running lengthwise rather than across.

mantle Section of the Earth's interior that comprises molten rock.

marine inundation/transgression Rising of sea level or sinking of land resulting in flooding by the ocean.

melanism Condition resulting in increase of dark pigments.

migrant Moving from one place to another, usually over long distances.

native Naturally occurring or originating in a certain area.

naturalized Refers to organism that has been introduced to a region where it is not indigenous, and lives wild there.

neurotoxic Relates to venom or poison that impacts nerves or nervous tissues.

nocturnal Active mostly during the night.

ocelli Small markings that are usually bright in the middle with darker edges.

oviparous Reproducing by laying eggs.

pākihi Wetland vegetation or habitat often associated with West Coast of the South Island of Aotearoa/New Zealand.

pelagic Relating to the open ocean or water column.

plastron Hard, bony underside of a turtle's shell.

plate boundary Point where two tectonic plates meet.

Pliocene (Epoch) Period in geologic time between 5.3 and 2.6 million years ago.

posterior Rear of an organism or part of an organism.

precloacal pores Femoral pores on the underside of the hindlegs that secrete a waxy substance

precipitous Extremely high or steep.

quadrennially Refers to process or event that takes place approximately once every four years.

rare Existing in low numbers, in few locations, and/or very difficult to find, resulting in an increased risk of extinction.

rock bluff Steep ledge or cliff made of rock.

rocky fellfield Habitat that usually occurs beneath or near tops of hills and mountains, and is dominated by scattered rocks of various sizes (may have a variety of vegetation types).

schist Type of metamorphic rock that is usually highly fractured and foliated.

scree Sloping habitat that is an aggregation of rocks that are loose and shift when stood on by a human.

scrubland Habitat that is usually quite open and comprises predominantly shrubs, grasses and low-growing trees (may include kānuka canopy).

snout–vent length (SVL) Measurement taken from tip of snout to cloacal vent on ventral surface of an organism.

speckles Markings that are usually fine or circular.

subduction Crust of one tectonic plate edge moving downwards into the Earth's mantle beneath another tectonic plate.

sympatric Refers to organism that occupies geographical area that overlaps geographical area of another organism.

talus Sloping habitat that is an aggregation of rocks that are not as large as those in a boulderfield or as small as those in scree, and generally do not move when stood on by a human.

taxon (pl. taxa) Unit used in science of classification of organisms.

taxonomy Science of classification of biological organisms.

temperate Relates to region characterized by mild climate.

thermoregulation Biological mechanism for retaining stable internal body temperature.

tor Large, freestanding rock outcrop.

transverse bands Markings that extend across an animal, rather than lengthwise.

tubercule Small, rounded lump or protuberance.

tussockland Specific habitat comprising predominantly tussock.

vagrant Wandering between places, usually not remaining in one area for extended periods.

ventral Relating to surfaces on underside of an animal's body.

vicariant Origins of an animal due to environmental fragmentation such as plate tectonics/ continental drift, rather than long-distance dispersal.

viviparous Refers to animal that gives birth to live young, which have developed inside the mother's body.

xanthochromism Condition resulting in inhibition of most pigments other than brown, orange and yellow, resulting in an excessive yellow appearance.

Tuatara ■ *Sphenodon punctatus* ≤280mm SVL

DESCRIPTION Largest reptile in Aotearoa/New Zealand and one of the most ancient reptiles in the world. Dorsal surface slate-grey, olive-green or orange-yellow, with a beautiful soft, white-spined crest (hence the Māori name meaning 'peaks on the back'). Often bears pale blotches or speckles and lumpy tubercules. Crest larger in males than females, and used in mating and territorial displays. Ventral surface pale grey (uniform or lightly speckled). **DISTRIBUTION** Historically, widespread throughout Aotearoa/New Zealand but now restricted to a range of offshore islands and several ecosanctuaries. **HABITS AND HABITAT** Cathemeral. Inhabits native forest, scrubland, grassland, beaches and seabird burrows. Basks and forages near burrow entrance, among leaf litter, dense vegetation, and rocks and logs, or on trees. Known to share burrows with seabirds, but often preys on chicks and eggs. Lays up to 18 eggs (which are buried in soil for up to 16 months). Offspring sex is largely determined by temperature-induced physiological mechanisms. May take more than a decade to reach sexual maturity and can live for over 100 years. **CONSERVATION** Relict. Very vulnerable to mammalian predation. Has greatly benefited from numerous translocations, monitoring and predator control. This, combined with its evolutionary significance, makes it one of Aotearoa's/New Zealand's most iconic native species.

Harlequin Gecko ▪ *Tukutuku rakiurae* ≤71mm SVL

DESCRIPTION Gorgeous, exquisitely patterned and distinct. Dorsal surface bears intricate 'tukutuku' pattern (hence the Māori genus name meaning 'decorative lattice work'), with complex colour combinations of brown, olive, green, grey, black, yellow, white, orange or red. Ventral surface variable but often grey-brown (uniform or speckled). Inside of mouth and tongue grey, blue and/or pink-purple. **DISTRIBUTION** Southern Rakiura/Stewart Island. **HABITS AND HABITAT** Cathemeral. Inhabits lowland and subalpine herbfield, wetland, shrubland and rocky fellfield. Often found in mānuka, moss, cushion plants, tangle ferns, *Olearia*, *Astelia*, wire rush and sedges. Basks, forages and takes shelter in low-growing, dense vegetation, on or under rocks or the ground. **CONSERVATION** Nationally Endangered.

James Reardon

Aupōuri Gecko ▪ *Naultinus flavirictus* ≤84mm SVL

DESCRIPTION The northernmost green gecko in Aotearoa/New Zealand; individuals at northern extent of their range are generally elegant and gracile (typically ≤70mm SVL), whereas individuals at southern extent of their range are generally larger and more robust (typically ≤80mm SVL). Dorsal surface vibrant green, typically with pairs of white or yellow blotches (may bear longitudinal stripes). Ventral surface uniform pale green (may be flushed blue in males). Inside of mouth pink-lilac or mauve and yellow-orange near edges of gums (hence the Latin species name meaning yellow lips) with red tongue. Individuals at southern extent of their range often lack yellow lips. Resembles the Northland Green Gecko (opposite), but the Aupōuri Gecko is smaller (typically ≤80mm v ≥95mm SVL), and typically has yellow-orange lip edges and a mauve mouth (v blue). **DISTRIBUTION** Aupōuri Peninsula. **HABITS AND HABITAT** Diurnal or cathemeral. Inhabits scrubland and coastal forest. Often found in trees like mānuka, kānuka, other dense vegetation and grasses. Basks, forages and takes shelter in dense vegetation. **CONSERVATION** Declining.

Northern individual

Southern individual

Northland Green Gecko ■ *Naultinus grayii* ≤100mm SVL

DESCRIPTION Large, beautiful and vibrant. Dorsal surface bright green, often with paired, pale green, yellow, grey or white blotches (may bear speckles and longitudinal stripes). Ventral surface uniform pale green or yellow-green. Inside of mouth deep blue with red tongue. Resembles the Aupōuri Gecko (opposite), but the Northland Green Gecko lacks yellow-orange colouration along lip, has a darker blue mouth (v mauve) and is generally larger (typically ≥80mm v ≤70mm SVL). Resembles the Elegant Gecko, but the Northland Green Gecko typically has flat canthal scales (v semi-domed) and red tongue (v blue-black).
DISTRIBUTION Tai Tokerau/Northland from Houhora Harbour to Te Pēwhairangi/ Bay of Islands. **HABITS AND HABITAT** Diurnal or cathemeral. Inhabits coastal and lowland forest, and scrubland. Often found in trees like mānuka, kānuka and other dense vegetation. Basks, forages and takes shelter in dense vegetation. **CONSERVATION** Declining.

Elegant Gecko ■ *Naultinus elegans* ≤75mm SVL

DESCRIPTION Gracile, elegant and widespread. Dorsal surface bright green or yellow (rarely), often with paired pale green, yellow, white or pink blotches (may bear longitudinal stripes). Ventral surface uniform pale green, pale blue or white. Inside of mouth dark blue with dark blue-black tongue. Resembles the Northland Green Gecko (p. 27), but the Elegant Gecko is smaller (typically ≤75mm v ≥80mm SVL), and has a blue-black tongue (v red). Resembles the Barking Gecko (opposite), but the Elegant Gecko is typically more slender, has less granular skin, and the soles of its feet are grey-green (v yellow). **DISTRIBUTION** Widespread throughout central and upper North Island from Whanganui to East Cape through to the Te Pēwhairangi/Bay of Islands. Present on some large offshore islands. **HABITS AND HABITAT** Diurnal or cathemeral. Inhabits coastal and lowland forest, and scrubland. Often found in trees like mānuka, kānuka and other dense vegetation. Basks, forages and takes shelter in dense vegetation. **CONSERVATION** Declining. Present in several ecosanctuaries and on some predator-free islands.

Barking Gecko ■ *Naultinus punctatus* ≤95mm SVL

DESCRIPTION Large, robust and striking. Dorsal surface green or yellow (rarely), often with paired yellow or light blue-green blotches (may bear speckles and longitudinal stripes). Males often have lateral surfaces and limbs flushed blue or white. Ventral surface uniform pale green. Inside of mouth bright blue with dark blue-black tongue. Resembles the Elegant Gecko (opposite), but the Barking Gecko is more robust, has more granular scales and the soles of its feet are yellow (v pale green or grey-white). **DISTRIBUTION** Widespread in southeastern North Island from East Cape to Whanganui southwards to Te Whanganui-a-Tara/Wellington. Present on several predator-free islands. **HABITS AND HABITAT** Diurnal or cathemeral. Inhabits coastal and lowland forest, and scrubland. Often found in trees like mānuka, kānuka and other dense vegetation. Basks, forages and takes shelter in dense vegetation. May lunge forwards and vocalize (hence its colloquial name). **CONSERVATION** Declining. Present in multiple ecosanctuaries and has been translocated to several offshore islands.

Male

Female

Marlborough Green Gecko ■ *Naultinus manukanus* ≤81mm SVL

DESCRIPTION Stout, beautiful and often bears raised conical scales. Dorsal surface green (rarely yellow), often with paired pale green, white or yellow markings. Raised or enlarged conical scales typically present on snout and/or dorsolateral surfaces. Ventral surface uniform pale blue-green, blue-white (in males), or yellow-green (in females). Inside of mouth mauve with pink tongue. Resembles the Rough Gecko (opposite), but the Marlborough Green Gecko has a mauve mouth (v dark blue purple), is typically less colourful or patterned (especially on the ventral surface), and large conical scales are generally restricted to the head and dorsolateral surfaces (v all over). **DISTRIBUTION** Marlborough north of the Wairau River westwards to Bryant Range, near Whakatū/Nelson. Present on various offshore islands in Marlborough Sounds.

HABITS AND HABITAT Diurnal or cathemeral. Inhabits coastal and lowland forest, and scrubland. Often found in trees or shrubs like mānuka, kānuka, tauhinu, mingimingi and other dense vegetation. Basks, forages and takes shelter in dense vegetation.

CONSERVATION Declining. Seldom seen on the mainland South Island, but surveys and monitoring have indicated that it is highly abundant on some offshore islands. Has been translocated to two additional offshore islands.

Male

Xanthochromic yellow morph

Nick Harker

Rough Gecko ▪ *Naultinus rudis* ≤77mm SVL

DESCRIPTION Stunning, variable and bears highly distinctive raised conical scales. Dorsal surface green, olive or grey-brown, with pale green, yellow or white markings (may bear irregular longitudinal stripes). Ventral surface

Grey male

blotched pale green, brown or grey. Inside of mouth dark blue or purple with dark blue or purple tongue (tongue-tip may be a lighter colour). Resembles the Marlborough Green Gecko (opposite), but the Rough Gecko is more robust, and has more prominent colouration and raised conical scales over the entire body (v mostly the head and dorsolateral region). Resembles the Starred Gecko (p. 32), but the Rough Gecko bears raised conical scales. **DISTRIBUTION** Southern Marlborough to northern Waitaha/ Canterbury east of the Main Divide. **HABITS AND HABITAT** Diurnal or cathemeral. Inhabits forest and scrubland (from the coast to subalpine areas). Often found in trees or shrubs like mānuka, kānuka, mingimingi, matagouri and other dense vegetation. Basks, forages and takes shelter in dense vegetation. **CONSERVATION** Nationally Endangered. Like most green gecko species, has suffered from extensive habitat modification, and introduced mammalian, avian and vespine predators.

Starred Gecko ■ *Naultinus stellatus* ≤81mm SVL

DESCRIPTION Incredibly striking and highly variable. Dorsal surface green, brown, white or grey (rarely yellow), typically with large, paired, white, green or yellow blotches (may bear speckles and irregular longitudinal stripes). Northern populations (for instance at Te One-tahua/Farewell Spit) are often uniform green (or with subtle markings), whereas southern populations (for example at Nelson Lakes) are usually strikingly marked and colourful. Ventral surface pale grey, green, green-blue, white or brown (uniform or speckled). Inside of mouth pale blue, lilac or pink, with orange-red tongue. Resembles the West Coast Green Gecko (opposite), but the Starred Gecko has a lavender or pink mouth with orange-red tongue (v black or dark blue mouth and tongue). Resembles the Marlborough Green Gecko (p. 30) and Rough Gecko (p. 31), but the Starred Gecko does not have enlarged conical scales. **DISTRIBUTION** Maitai Valley westwards through Whakatū/Nelson and Tasman regions, southwards to Nelson Lakes. **HABITS AND HABITAT** Diurnal or cathemeral. Inhabits forest and scrubland (from the coast to subalpine areas). Often found in trees or shrubs like mānuka, kānuka, matagouri, mingimingi and other dense vegetation.

Basks, forages and takes shelter in dense vegetation. **CONSERVATION** Nationally Vulnerable. Has suffered from extensive habitat modification, and introduced mammalian, avian and vespine predators.

Nelson Lakes (female)

Nelson Lakes (male)

Nelson Lakes (subadult)

West Coast Green Gecko ■ *Naultinus tuberculatus* ≤85mm SVL

DESCRIPTION Lesser-known green gecko with brilliant moss-like patterning. Dorsal surface green or brown (rarely yellow) with green-yellow diamonds (may bear speckles, pale green mid-dorsal stripe and longitudinal stripes). Ventral surface typically pale green (uniform or speckled). Inside of mouth blue with dark blue or black tongue. Resembles the Starred Gecko (opposite), but the West Coast Green Gecko has a blue mouth with dark blue or black tongue (v yellow or red-orange). Resembles the Rough Gecko (p. 31), but the West Coast Green Gecko does not bear enlarged conical scales. **DISTRIBUTION** Lewis Pass westwards, south of Stockton to Hokitika. May occur further south. **HABITS AND HABITAT** Diurnal or cathemeral. Inhabits scrubland, forest, rocky shrubland and fernland (from the coast to subalpine areas). Often found in trees or shrubs like mānuka, kānuka, matagouri, low-growing shrubs and other dense vegetation. Basks, forages and takes shelter in dense vegetation. May seek refuge under rocks. **CONSERVATION** Nationally Vulnerable.

Lewis Pass individual

West Coast (female)

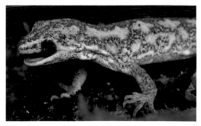

West Coast (male)

Jewelled Gecko ■ *Naultinus gemmeus* ≤90mm

DESCRIPTION The southernmost green gecko in Aotearoa/ New Zealand; striking and iconic. Dorsal surface typically bright green (very rarely yellow) with white, yellow, green, pinkish or brown diamonds or blotches and/or longitudinal stripes. Most males in mid to north Waitaha/Canterbury (including Te Pātaka-o-Rākaihautū/Banks Peninsula), and some in Te Manahuna/ Mackenzie District, are grey-brown in colouration. Ventral surface green, green-yellow, grey or pale brown (uniform or blotched). Inside of mouth pink or dark blue-purple with pink, orange or dark blue-black tongue. Resembles the Rough Gecko (p. 31), but the Jewelled Gecko does not have raised conical scales. **DISTRIBUTION** Relatively widespread from Ashley River in Canterbury to Murihiku/Southland. Present on Te Pātaka-o-Rākaihautū/Banks Peninsula and some islands in Te Ara-a-Kiwi/Foveaux Strait (on Whenua Hou/Codfish Island, lacks bright markings). **HABITS AND HABITAT** Diurnal or cathemeral. Inhabits scrubland, forest and tussockland (from the coast to subalpine and alpine areas, ≤1,300m). Often found in trees or shrubs like beech, mānuka, kānuka, mingimingi, matagouri, snow tussock and other dense vegetation. Basks, forages and takes shelter in dense vegetation. May seek refuge under rocks or the ground during winter. **CONSERVATION** Declining. Some populations are regularly monitored, and many new ones have been discovered. Has been translocated to two ecosanctuaries. Fires, habitat modification and poaching are major threats to several populations.

Muaūpoko/Otago Peninsula individual

Te Pātaka-o-Rākaihautū/Banks Peninsula (male)

Central Otago individual

Northern Striped Gecko ■ *Toropuku inexpectatus* ≤95mm SVL

DESCRIPTION Gorgeous, elusive and distinct. Dorsal surface tan, golden-brown or reddish, with distinctive dorsolateral stripes and exquisite woodgrain pattern. Ventral surface pale sandy colour (uniform or lightly speckled). Inside of mouth and tongue pink. **DISTRIBUTION** Only known from Te Tara-o-te-Ika a Māui/Coromandel Peninsula. May have been more widespread historically and may still exist elsewhere. **HABITS AND HABITAT** Nocturnal or cathemeral. Inhabits lowland scrubland and forest. Often found in trees, shrubs, kiekie, vines, flaxes and ferns. Forages and takes shelter on trees, among dense vegetation or under loose bark. May bask cryptically. Known to be an agile climber and to leap with precision. **CONSERVATION**

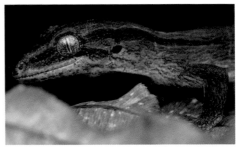

Nationally Vulnerable. Discovered in 1997, when an individual was found inside a Coromandel township home. Once thought to be one of the rarest geckos in the world. However, surveys and monitoring have indicated that it is abundant in at least one location. Intensive predator control may be highly important for the persistence of the species.

▪ GECKOS ▪

Southern Striped Gecko ▪ *Toropuku stephensi* ≤85mm SVL

DESCRIPTION Beautiful, slender and distinct. Dorsal surface tan, golden-brown, yellowish or reddish, with distinctive dorsolateral stripes and exquisite woodgrain pattern. Ventral surface pale sandy colour (uniform or lightly speckled). Inside of mouth and tongue pink (edges of mouth may be orange). **DISTRIBUTION** Known from several islands in Raukawa Moana/Cook Strait and Marlborough Sounds. May have been more widespread historically and could still exist elsewhere. **HABITS AND HABITAT** Nocturnal or cathemeral. Inhabits coastal and lowland scrubland, flaxland and forest. Often found in trees, shrubs, kiekie, vines, flaxes and ferns. Forages and takes shelter on trees, among dense vegetation, or under rocks or loose bark. May bask cryptically. Known to move quickly and leap with precision. **CONSERVATION** Nationally Vulnerable. Has been translocated to one additional predator-free island. In 2020 a third natural population was discovered on an island in the far eastern Marlborough Sounds.

Nick Harker

Ngahere Gecko ■ *Mokopirirakau* 'Southern North Island' ≤85mm SVL

DESCRIPTION Closely resembles the Forest Gecko (opposite) but is deeply divergent from all other *Mokopirirakau* species. Dorsal surface grey, brown or olive, with irregular grey, brown, olive, yellow-cream, yellow, orange-brown or orange markings (may bear speckles). Ventral surface pale grey, cream or white (uniform or speckled). Inside of mouth and tongue bright orange or yellow. Resembles the Forest Gecko, but the Ngahere Gecko typically has a shorter snout and its dorsal markings are usually broken up across the mid-dorsal line in two rows (v continuous). **DISTRIBUTION** Widespread in southeastern North Island from East Cape, Tūranga-nui-a-Kiwa/Gisborne and Te Matau-a-Māui/Hawkes Bay, southwards through Tararua Ranges to Te Whanganui-a-Tara/Wellington. Present on Kāpiti Island, Matiu/Somes and Te Mana-o-Kupe-ki-Aotearoa/Mana Island. **HABITS AND HABITAT** Nocturnal or cathemeral. Inhabits coastal and lowland scrubland, and forest (may exist above tree line). Forages and takes shelter on trees, among dense vegetation, clay banks, under loose bark, or on or under rocks and logs. May bask cryptically. **CONSERVATION** Declining. Present in several ecosanctuaries and on offshore islands.

Forest Gecko ▪ *Mokopirirakau granulatus* ≤98mm SVL

DESCRIPTION The most widespread species of *Mokopirirakau* in Aotearoa/New Zealand; large and beautiful. Dorsal surface grey, brown or olive, with 'W'-shaped markings and grey, brown, olive, yellow, cream or orange blotches (may bear speckles). Ventral surface pale grey or cream (uniform or speckled). Inside of mouth bright orange or yellow with orange or red tongue. Resembles the Ngahere Gecko (opposite), but the Forest Gecko typically has a longer snout and its dorsal markings are usually continuous across the mid-dorsal line (v broken up). Resembles the Ōkārito/Broad-cheeked Gecko (p. 42), but morphological differences are poorly understood. **DISTRIBUTION** Widespread in the North Island from southern Pēwhairangi/ Bay of Islands to Taranaki. Possibly exists as far east as East Cape. Widespread in the South Island from Marlborough through to Tasman, southwards to Lewis Pass and Westland. Present on several offshore Islands in the North Island and Marlborough Sounds. **HABITS AND HABITAT** Nocturnal or cathemeral. Inhabits scrubland, forest, creviced rock outcrops, and rocky scrub from the coast to alpine areas. Forages and takes shelter on trees, among dense vegetation, under loose bark or on or under rocks and logs. May bask cryptically. **CONSERVATION** Declining. Present in several ecosanctuaries. Genetic analyses have revealed that the recently rediscovered 'Cupola Gecko' is a distinctive-looking population of this species.

Ben Barr

Nelson Lakes individual

Westland individual

Waikato individual

Black-eyed Gecko ▪ *Mokopirirakau kahutarae* ≤96mm SVL

DESCRIPTION Large, cryptic and bears distinctive black eyes. Dorsal surface grey or olive-grey with pale markings (may bear speckles). Ventral surface grey-white (uniform or lightly speckled). Inside of mouth pale red or pink, with pinkish, red or orange tongue. Resembles the Hura Te Ao Gecko (opposite), but the Black-eyed Gecko typically has a less prominently speckled dorsal surface, vivid black eyes (v dark brown) and a more prominent brillar fold/supraciliaries (eyebrow fringe scales).
DISTRIBUTION Known from Tasman, Whakatū/Nelson-Marlborough and Kaikōura. May exist in Waitaha/Canterbury.
HABITS AND HABITAT Nocturnal. Inhabits alpine creviced rock outcrops, rock walls or extensive tor systems. Occupies the highest known elevation of any Aotearoa/New Zealand gecko (≤2,200m). Forages and takes shelter on rock surfaces, in deep crevices or under rocks (rarely).
CONSERVATION Nationally Vulnerable.

Hura Te Ao Gecko ▪ *Mokopirirakau galaxias* ≤88mm SVL

DESCRIPTION Discovered in 2018; striking and cryptic. Dorsal surface olive-grey or olive-green, with galaxy-like pattern comprising small white spots. Ventral surface pale grey and speckled. Inside of mouth bright orange and pink, with pinkish tongue (tongue-base may bear orange-yellow accents). Resembles the Black-eyed Gecko (opposite), but the Hura Te Ao Gecko typically has a more prominently speckled dorsal surface, dark brown eyes (v vivid black), and highly conspicuous upper eye margins (v hidden), with reduced brillar fold/supraciliaries (eyebrow fringe scales). **DISTRIBUTION** Only known from two mountain ranges in Oteake Conservation Park, North Otago. May exist elsewhere. **HABITS AND HABITAT** Nocturnal. Inhabits alpine creviced rock outcrops, rock walls, extensive tor systems, boulderfield and talus. Forages and takes shelter on rock surfaces, in deep crevices, boulderfield, talus or under rocks (rarely). **CONSERVATION** Nationally Endangered. Until late 2020, was only known from an area of less than 2ha. However, surveys have identified it occupying boulderfield and talus at several sites across two mountain ranges.

Ōkārito/Broad-cheeked Gecko ■ *Mokopirirakau 'Ōkārito'* ≤90mm SVL

DESCRIPTION Obscure and seldom seen. Dorsal surface brown, grey or olive, with irregular grey, brown, yellow-cream, yellow, pink or orange markings (may bear speckles). Ventral surface grey or brown, with blotches (may bear cream or pale yellow markings). Inside of mouth and tongue bright orange. Resembles the Forest Gecko (p. 39), but morphological differences are poorly understood. Resembles the Cascade Gecko (p. 44), but the Ōkārito/Broad-cheeked Gecko is typically more robust, with a broader head and more heavily speckled ventral surface. Resembles the Open Bay Islands Gecko (opposite), but the Ōkārito/Broad-cheeked Gecko is typically much darker (with different dorsal pattern) and has larger scales. **DISTRIBUTION** Known from near Harihari in Westland southwards to Paringa River. May occur further south. **HABITS AND HABITAT** Nocturnal or cathemeral. Inhabits scrubland, pākihi, native forest, alpine and subalpine rocky scrubland, and boulderfield. Forages and takes shelter on trees, among dense vegetation, boulderfield, talus, in crevices, under loose bark, or on or under rocks. May bask cryptically. **CONSERVATION** Nationally Vulnerable. Until recently, very few records of this species existed. However, surveys and monitoring have revealed new populations and monitoring is being conducted regularly.

Open Bay Islands Gecko ■ *Mokopirirakau* 'Open Bay Islands' ≤80mm SVL

DESCRIPTION Possibly the smallest species of *Mokopirirakau* in Aotearoa/New Zealand; gracile and unique. Dorsal surface light brown, olive, olive-grey or reddish (in alpine populations), typically with pale markings and pale dorsolateral stripes connected by transverse bands. Ventral surface uniform cream. Inside of mouth and tongue bright orange. Resembles the Cascade Gecko (p. 44), but morphological differences are poorly understood in alpine and subalpine populations; the Open Bay Islands Gecko typically has finer scales (v larger and more granular). **DISTRIBUTION** Known from Taumaka Island in Open Bay Islands and the adjacent mainland. **HABITS AND HABITAT** Nocturnal or cathemeral. Inhabits coastal forest, scrubland, boulderfield and rocky herbfield or tussockland in alpine and subalpine areas. Forages and takes shelter on trees, among dense vegetation, boulderfield or talus, in crevices, under loose bark, or on or under rocks. May bask cryptically. **CONSERVATION** Nationally Endangered. Until 2021 was only known from Taumaka Island. However, recent surveys have identified an alpine population on the adjacent mainland.

Alpine individual (Mainand)

Marieke Lettink

Cascade Gecko ■ *Mokopirirakau* 'Cascades' ≤95mm SVL

DESCRIPTION Highly variable, cryptic and beautifully patterned. Dorsal surface brown, grey-brown, grey or orange, with conspicuous reddish, mustard-yellow, cream, brown or grey markings (may bear speckles and irregular longitudinal stripes). Ventral surface grey or brown and typically speckled. Inside of mouth and tongue bright orange. Resembles the Tākitimu Gecko (p. 47), but morphological differences are poorly understood; the Cascade gecko typically has an orange tongue (v often pink and/or grey). Resembles the Open Bay Islands Gecko (p. 43), but morphological differences are poorly understood in alpine and subalpine populations; the Cascade Gecko typically has larger, more granular scales (v finer). **DISTRIBUTION** Relatively widespread in southern Westland and northern Fiordland. **HABITS AND HABITAT** Nocturnal or cathemeral. Inhabits creviced rock walls, rocky shrubland, herbfield, boulderfield and forest (few records exist from forest). Occupies extreme high-altitude (≤1,800m) habitats prone to avalanches, rock falls and intense weather. Forages and takes shelter on trees, among dense vegetation, boulderfield,

talus, in crevices, under loose bark, or on or under rocks. May bask cryptically. Females living in alpine areas have extended pregnancies, lasting two years or more. Known to leap off sheer cliffs and land in shrubs to evade threats. **CONSERVATION** Declining. Population monitoring is being conducted.

Orange-spotted Gecko ▪ *Mokopirirakau* 'Roys Peak' ≤93mm SVL

DESCRIPTION Gorgeous, highly variable and often bears brilliant orange spots. Dorsal surface grey, brown, olive-brown, pinkish-brown or orange, with markings that are similar in colour, cream or black (may bear speckles and longitudinal stripes). Ventral surface grey, pinkish or pale orange (uniform or speckled). Inside of mouth and tongue bright orange or yellow. Resembles the Tākitimu Gecko (p. 47), but morphological differences are poorly understood; the Orange-spotted Gecko has an orange tongue (v often pink and/or grey). Resembles the Cascade Gecko (opposite), but morphological differences are poorly understood; the Orange-spotted Gecko typically has broader toes. **DISTRIBUTION** Relatively widespread in western Central Otago to North Otago and Queenstown Lakes area. **HABITS AND HABITAT** Nocturnal or cathemeral. Inhabits high-altitude (1,100–1,800m) alpine and subalpine creviced rock outcrops, rocky shrubland, boulderfield, talus, scree and rocky tussockland. Forages and takes shelter among dense vegetation, boulderfield, talus, in crevices, or on rocks. May bask cryptically. May exist in forest at lower elevations, but such habitats are rare across its range now. Has been found coexisting with the Hura Te Ao Gecko (p. 41) in North Otago. **CONSERVATION** Declining. Previously thought to be endangered, but surveys and regular monitoring have indicated that it is more abundant and widespread than previously thought.

Tautuku Gecko ■ *Mokopirirakau* 'Southern Forest' ≤91mm SVL

DESCRIPTION Beautifully coloured, highly variable and occasionally possesses brilliant blue eyes. Dorsal surface grey, brown, olive, yellowish or reddish, often with highly contrasting yellowish, reddish, grey or olive markings. Ventral surface cream, grey or yellowish and blotched. Inside of mouth bright orange with orange, pinkish or reddish tongue. Resembles the Tākitimu Gecko (opposite), but the Tautuku Gecko often bears yellow markings and has an intact tail equal to or longer than its body length (v equal to or shorter). **DISTRIBUTION** Known from the Catlins in south-east Otago, to Murihiku/Southland. May exist elsewhere, as museum specimens from Aparima/Riverton exist. **HABITS AND HABITAT** Nocturnal or cathemeral.

Inhabits coastal and lowland podocarp forest, scrubland, and possibly beech forest. Forages and takes shelter on trees, among dense vegetation, under loose bark, or on or under rocks and logs. May bask cryptically. **CONSERVATION** Declining. Was thought to be endangered, but surveys and regular monitoring have identified that it is very cryptic and can be difficult to find, rather than highly threatened.

Tākitimu Gecko ■ *Mokopirirakau cryptozoicus* ≤87mm SVL

DESCRIPTION Stunning, elusive and seldom seen. Dorsal surface slate-grey or olive, with red, orange, cream-yellow, grey or purple-grey markings (may bear speckles and irregular longitudinal stripes). Ventral surface pale grey or cream-yellow (uniform or blotched). Inside of mouth bright orange with pink or grey tongue (tongue-tip may be grey). Resembles the Cascade Gecko (p. 44), but morphological differences are poorly understood; the Tākitimu Gecko often has a pink and/or grey tongue (v orange). Resembles the Orange-spotted Gecko (p. 45), but morphological differences are poorly understood; the Tākitimu Gecko has a mostly pink and/or grey tongue (v usually bright orange) and an intact tail shorter than its SVL (v equal to or longer). Resembles the Tautuku Gecko (opposite), but the Tākitimu Gecko is not known to bear bright yellow markings (only pale cream-yellow), and has an intact tail shorter than its body length (v equal to or longer). **DISTRIBUTION** Southwestern Otago to Western Murihiku/Southland and South Fiordland. Present on Mauīkatau/Resolution Island. **HABITS AND HABITAT** Nocturnal or cathemeral. Inhabits high-altitude (≤1,450m) creviced rock outcrops, rock walls, alpine scree, rocky herbfield and lowland forest. Forages and takes shelter on trees, among dense vegetation, scree, talus, in crevices, under loose bark, or on or under rocks. May bask cryptically. **CONSERVATION** Nationally Vulnerable. Very few records of the species exist, but they are distributed over a large geographical area.

Cloudy Gecko ■ *Mokopirirakau nebulosus* ≤90mm SVL

DESCRIPTION Seldom seen and has a unique cloudy appearance. Dorsal surface brown, grey, olive-grey, dark green or pink-brown, with pale grey or yellow markings (may bear speckles and irregular longitudinal stripes). Ventral surface grey or cream (uniform or speckled). Inside of mouth bright yellow or orange with orange or pinkish tongue (tongue-tip may be grey). **DISTRIBUTION** Known from mainland Rakiura/Stewart Island and surrounding islands such as Whenua Hou/Codfish Island, and Tītī/Muttonbird Islands. **HABITS AND HABITAT** Nocturnal or cathemeral. Inhabits scrubland, forest and rocky environments (from the coast to montane and subalpine areas). One population has been recorded at a supralittoral barren rock stack with little to no vegetation. Forages and takes shelter on trees, among dense vegetation, under loose bark, or on or under rocks and logs. May bask cryptically. **CONSERVATION** Relict. Very few records of it exist on Stewart Island, possibly due to the prevalence of three rat species. Surveys and monitoring have indicated that it is present on multiple islands surrounding Stewart Island and can reach high densities in the absence of introduced mammalian predators.

James Reardon

Pacific Gecko ▪ *Dactylocnemis pacificus* ≤80mm SVL

DESCRIPTION Gorgeous, skittish and highly variable. Dorsal surface brown, grey or olive, with pale markings (may bear speckles and dorsolateral stripes). Nape may be mustard coloured (this colour may extend elsewhere on the body). Ventral surface pale grey or brown (uniform or speckled and may be flushed yellow). Inside of mouth and tongue pink. Resembles the Raukawa Gecko (p. 57), but the Pacific Gecko has rostral scale in broad contact with nostrils (v excluded). Resembles the Forest Gecko (p. 39), but the Pacific Gecko bears distinctive blotches or dorsolateral stripes (v thin, 'W'-shaped markings), and has a pink mouth and tongue (v orange or orange-yellow mouth and red tongue). **DISTRIBUTION** Te Pēwhairangi/Bay of Islands to Whanganui. Present on various offshore islands in northern extent of range. However, northernmost extent of range uncertain. **HABITS AND HABITAT** Nocturnal or cathemeral. Inhabits a range of coastal and lowland environments. Forages and takes shelter on trees, clay banks, among dense vegetation, leaf litter, under loose bark, in crevices, or on or under rocks and logs. May bask cryptically. **CONSERVATION** Not Threatened. Infrequently seen on the mainland but has been translocated to several predator-free islands.

Matapia Gecko ■ *Dactylocnemis* 'Matapia Island' ≤*60mm SVL*

DESCRIPTION Small, gracile and beautiful. Dorsal surface golden-brown, brown, dark olive or grey, with pale dorsolateral stripes (may bear speckles and blotches). Ventral surface cream (uniform or speckled). Inside of mouth pale pink, with dark grey and/or pink tongue (tongue-tip may be grey). Resembles the Te Paki Gecko (opposite), but the Matapia Gecko is smaller (typically ≤60mm v ≥70mm SVL) and has broader toes. Resembles the Raukawa Gecko (p. 57), but the Te Paki Gecko has rostral scale in broad contact with nostrils (v excluded).

DISTRIBUTION Aupōuri Peninsula, Karikari Peninsula and multiple offshore islands in these areas. **HABITS AND HABITAT** Nocturnal or cathemeral. Inhabits coastal and lowland scrubland, and forest. Forages and takes shelter on trees, clay banks, among dense vegetation, leaf litter, under loose bark, in crevices, or on or under rocks and logs. May bask cryptically. **CONSERVATION** Declining.

Te Paki Gecko ■ *Dactylocnemis* 'North Cape' ≤84mm SVL

DESCRIPTION Graceful and beautifully patterned. Dorsal surface grey, brown or olive, with pale markings (may be speckled and bear dorsolateral stripes). Nape may be mustard coloured. Ventral surface pale grey or white (uniform or speckled). Throat may be flushed orange. Inside of mouth and tongue pink (tongue-tip may be grey). Resembles the Matapia Gecko (opposite), but the Te Paki Gecko is larger (typically ≥70mm v ≤60mm SVL), darker, usually has blotches (v usually striped), and has longer distal phalanges and narrower toes. **DISTRIBUTION** Only known from Aupōuri Peninsula. **HABITS AND HABITAT** Nocturnal or cathemeral. Inhabits coastal and lowland scrubland, forest, and mangroves. Forages and takes shelter on trees, clay banks, among dense vegetation, leaf litter, under loose bark, in crevices, or on or under rocks and logs. May bask cryptically. **CONSERVATION** Declining.

Three Kings Gecko ■ *Dactylocnemis* 'Three Kings' 100mm SVL

DESCRIPTION One of the largest geckos in Aotearoa/New Zealand. Dorsal surface brown, grey or olive, with large pale markings (may bear speckles and dorsolateral stripes). Nape may be mustard coloured. Ventral surface uniform cream or pale brown. Inside of mouth and tongue pink (tongue-tip may be grey). **DISTRIBUTION** Manawatāwhi/Three Kings Islands. **HABITS AND HABITAT** Nocturnal or cathemeral. Inhabits scrubland and coastal forest. Forages and takes shelter on trees, clay banks, among dense vegetation, leaf litter, under loose bark, in crevices, or on or under rocks and logs. May bask cryptically. **CONSERVATION** Naturally Uncommon.

Dylan van Winkel

Poor Knights Gecko ■ *Dactylocnemis* 'Poor Knights' ≤95mm SVL

DESCRIPTION Robust, highly variable and often found in high densities. Dorsal surface brown, grey or olive, with large pale markings (may bear speckles and dorsolateral stripes). Nape may be mustard coloured. Ventral surface uniform pale grey or cream. Inside of mouth and tongue pink. Resembles the Northern Duvaucel's Gecko (p. 55), but the Poor Knights Gecko is smaller (typically ≤90mm v ≥110mm SVL), and usually has brown or olive-brown eyes (v brighter olive or green), and narrower toes. **DISTRIBUTION** Poor Knights Islands. **HABITS AND HABITAT** Nocturnal or cathemeral. Inhabits scrubland and coastal forest. Forages and takes shelter on trees, clay banks, among dense vegetation, leaf litter, under loose bark, in crevices, or on or under rocks and logs. May bask cryptically. Known to feed on fish regurgitated by seabirds. **CONSERVATION** Naturally Uncommon.

Dylan van Winkel

Mokohinau Gecko ▪ *Dactylocnemis* 'Mokohinau' ≤90mm SVL

DESCRIPTION Robust, alert and highly variable. Dorsal surface grey, brown or olive, with large pale markings (may bear speckles and dorsolateral stripes). Nape may be mustard coloured. Ventral surface uniform pale grey or cream. Inside of mouth and tongue pink (tongue-tip may be grey). Resembles the Northern Duvaucel's Gecko (opposite), but the Mokohinau Gecko is smaller (typically ≤90mm v ≥110mm SVL), and usually has brown or olive-brown eyes (v brighter olive or green), and narrower toes.

DISTRIBUTION
Mokohinau Islands. **HABITS AND HABITAT** Nocturnal or cathemeral. Inhabits scrubland, rocky cliffs, vineland, flaxland and coastal forest. Forages and takes shelter on trees, clay banks, among dense vegetation, leaf litter, under loose bark, in crevices, or on or under rocks and logs. May bask cryptically.
CONSERVATION Naturally Uncommon.

Dylan van Winkel

Northern Duvaucel's Gecko ■ *Hoplodactylus duvaucelii* ≤165mm SVL

DESCRIPTION Largest gecko in Aotearoa/New Zealand and one of the longest lived geckos in the world (captive individuals have exceeded 50 years). Dorsal surface grey, grey-brown or olive-brown, with pale markings. Ventral surface pale grey or cream (uniform or lightly speckled). Inside of mouth and tongue pink. Resembles allopatric Southern Duvaucel's Gecko (p. 56), but the Northern Duvaucel's Gecko is larger (110–165mm v 95–120mm SVL), has a longer snout, less pronounced brillar fold/supraciliaries (eyebrow fringe scales), and gradually smaller infralabial scales (v abruptly smaller following fourth infralabial scale). Juveniles resemble the Raukawa Gecko (p. 57) and Pacific Gecko ((p. 49), but the Northern Duvaucel's Gecko has longer distal phalanges and a proportionately larger head.

DISTRIBUTION Historically, widespread on the mainland North Island, but now mostly restricted to predator-free islands in the northern North Island. **HABITS AND HABITAT** Nocturnal or cathemeral. Inhabits scrubland, coastal forest and rocky shorelines. Forages and takes shelter on trees, clay banks, among dense vegetation and leaf litter, under loose bark, in crevices, or on or under rocks and logs. May bask cryptically. **CONSERVATION** Relict. Very vulnerable to mammalian predation. Has been captive bred and translocated to many predator-free islands and Tāwharanui Open Sanctuary on the mainland.

Southern Duvaucel's Gecko ▪ *Hoplodactylus duvaucelii* 'Southern'
≤120mm SVL

DESCRIPTION Second largest gecko in Aotearoa/New Zealand; beautiful and robust. Dorsal surface grey, brownish or olive-brown, with pale transverse markings (may bear speckles). Ventral surface pale grey or cream (uniform or speckled). Inside of mouth and tongue pink. Resembles allopatric Northern Duvaucel's Gecko (p. 55), but the Southern Duvaucel's Gecko is smaller (95–120mm v 110–165mm SVL), and has a shorter snout, more pronounced brillar fold/supraciliaries (eyebrow fringe scales), and abruptly smaller infralabial scales following the fourth infralabial scale (v gradually smaller infralabial scales). Juveniles resemble the Raukawa Gecko (opposite), but the Southern Duvaucel's Gecko has longer distal phalanges and a proportionately larger head. **DISTRIBUTION** Historically, widespread on the mainland South Island, but now restricted to predator-free islands in Raukawa Moana/Cook Strait and Marlborough Sounds. **HABITS AND HABITAT** Nocturnal or cathemeral. Inhabits scrubland and coastal forest. Forages and takes shelter on trees, clay banks, among dense vegetation and leaf litter, under loose bark, in crevices, or on or under rocks and logs. May bask cryptically. **CONSERVATION** Nationally Increasing. Has been translocated to several predator-free islands in Marlborough Sounds and Te Mana-o-Kupe-ki-Aotearoa/Mana Island near Te Whanganui-a-Tara/Wellington.

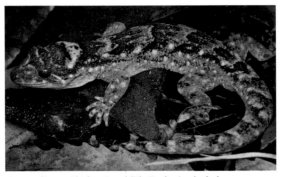

Tōtaranui/Queen Charlotte Sound (The Brothers) individual

Te Hoiere/Pelorus Sound individual

Nick Harker

Raukawa Gecko ■ *Woodworthia maculata* ≤89mm SVL

DESCRIPTION Highly variable, widespread and known to reach high densities in predator-free environments. Dorsal surface grey, brown or olive-brown, often with pale markings (may bear speckles and dorsolateral stripes). Ventral surface grey or brown (uniform or speckled). Inside of mouth and tongue pink (tongue-tip may be grey). Resembles the Goldstripe Gecko (p. 59), but the Raukawa Gecko is often darker, more mottled (v mostly uniform brown-gold, less mottled), and typically lacks smooth-edged dorsolateral stripes (which do not extend down tail). Raukawa Gecko typically also has a wider and blunter snout. Resembles the Minimac Gecko (p. 62), but the Raukawa Gecko is larger. Resembles the Pacific Gecko (p. 49), but the Raukawa Gecko has its rostral scale in narrow contact or excluded from nostrils (v in broad contact). **DISTRIBUTION** Widespread on eastern coastline of the North Island from southern Tai Tokerau/Northland through to Whanganui and Te Whanganui-a-Tara/Wellington. Occupies Whakatū/Nelson, Marlborough and Tasman in the South Island. Present on many offshore islands. **HABITS AND HABITAT** Nocturnal or cathemeral. Inhabits range of lowland and coastal environments. Forages and takes shelter on trees, clay banks, among dense vegetation and leaf litter, under loose bark, in crevices, or on or under rocks and logs. May bask cryptically. **CONSERVATION** Not Threatened. Has been translocated to multiple islands. Now relatively uncommon on the mainland in the northern North Island.

Muriwai Gecko ■ *Woodworthia* aff. *maculata* 'Muriwai' ≤69mm SVL

DESCRIPTION Beautifully speckled, seldom seen and distinctively striped. Dorsal surface grey or sandy-brown (may bear speckles, an indistinct mid-dorsal stripe and pale longitudinal stripes). Ventral surface uniform pale brown, grey or pink-brown. **DISTRIBUTION** West Coast of Auckland from Muriwai Beach to South Kaipara Head. Present on predator-free Oaia Island. May exist in western Tai Tokerau/Northland. **HABITS AND HABITAT** Nocturnal or cathemeral. Inhabits coastal dune systems, exotic pine forest, dense vegetation and creviced rock outcrops. Forages and takes shelter among low-growing vegetation, on sand, in crevices, under loose bark, or on or under rocks and driftwood. May bask cryptically. Highly energetic and known to leap with precision.

CONSERVATION Nationally Vulnerable. Was recognized as a potentially distinct taxon in 2013 and subsequently considered Nationally Critical. Surveys and monitoring have now identified it at several sites. However, it is still highly vulnerable to mammalian predators and habitat modification (particularly from fire, pedestrians, horses, motorbikes and four-wheel drive vehicles).

Tim Harker

Goldstripe Gecko ▪ *Woodworthia chrysosiretica* ≤80mm SVL

DESCRIPTION Striking and elegant. Dorsal surface golden-brown, olive-brown, brown or olive, typically with broad, smooth-edged dorsolateral stripes (which may be pale or bright cream-brown in colour). Ventral surface pale cream (uniform or speckled). Inside of mouth and tongue pink (tongue-tip may be red). Resembles the Pacific Gecko (p. 49), but the Goldstripe Gecko has rostral scale excluded from nostrils (v in broad contact). Resembles the Raukawa Gecko (p. 57), but the Goldstripe Gecko typically bears smooth-edged and continuous dorsolateral stripes that extend down tail (which are typically absent, less pronounced or do not extend down tail in the Raukawa Gecko). Goldstripe Gecko typically also has a narrower and more pointy snout. **DISTRIBUTION** Northern Taranaki to northern Whanganui. Present on Kāpiti and Te Mana-o-Kupe-ki-Aotearoa/Mana Island. May exist along coast south of Whanganui. **HABITS AND HABITAT** Nocturnal or cathemeral. Inhabits coastal and lowland scrubland, forest and boulder beaches. Forages and takes shelter on trees, among dense vegetation (particularly flaxes and *Astelia*), under loose bark, in crevices, or on or under rocks and logs. May bask cryptically. **CONSERVATION** Declining. Present on two predator-free offshore islands and in one mainland ecosanctuary.

Kahurangi Gecko ■ *Woodworthia* 'Mount Arthur' ≤68mm SVL

DESCRIPTION Small, attractive and seldom seen. Dorsal surface grey, brown or olive, with pale markings and speckles. Ventral surface pale grey (uniform or speckled). Inside of mouth and tongue pink (tongue-tip may be grey). Resembles the Sabine Gecko (opposite), but morphological differences are poorly understood. **DISTRIBUTION** Whakatū/Nelson-Tasman region from Mt Arthur westwards to Douglas Range. May occur elsewhere. **HABITS AND HABITAT** Nocturnal or cathemeral. Inhabits alpine and subalpine creviced rock outcrops, rocky scrubland, talus and scree. Forages and takes shelter among dense vegetation, boulderfield, talus and scree, in crevices, or on or under rocks (particularly marble slabs). May bask cryptically. **CONSERVATION** Declining.

Sabine Gecko ▪ *Woodworthia* 'Sabine' ≤71mm SVL

DESCRIPTION Discovered in 2021; small, beautiful and poorly understood (known from two individuals). Dorsal surface grey, brown or olive, with pale transverse bands and fine galaxy-like pattern consisting of small white spots. Ventral surface pale grey (uniform or speckled). Inside of mouth and tongue pink (tongue-tip may be grey). Resembles the Kahurangi Gecko (opposite), but morphological differences are poorly understood; the Sabine Gecko appears to have fine dorsal galaxy-like pattern (v uniform, speckled or with pale transverse markings). **DISTRIBUTION** Only known from Nelson Lakes National Park. May occur elsewhere. **HABITS AND HABITAT** Poorly known. However, it is most likely nocturnal or cathemeral with similar habits to related species, such as the Kahurangi Gecko. Inhabits alpine and subalpine rocky scrubland, talus and scree. Thought to forage and take shelter among dense vegetation, boulderfield, talus, scree, in crevices, or on or under rocks. May bask cryptically. **CONSERVATION** Data Deficient.

Minimac Gecko ■ *Woodworthia* 'Marlborough Mini' ≤65mm SVL

DESCRIPTION Petite, beautiful, and named after its small size and affinity to the Raukawa Gecko (p. 57). Dorsal surface grey, olive-grey or brown, with pale markings. Ventral surface pale brown or grey (uniform or speckled). Inside of mouth and tongue pink (tongue-tip may be grey). Resembles the Kaikouras Gecko (opposite), but the Minimac Gecko typically has a more coastal distribution, fewer lamellae (9–11 v 10–12) and broader toes. Resembles the Pygmy Gecko (p. 64), but the Minimac Gecko is larger. Resembles the Greywacke Gecko (p. 66), but the Minimac Gecko has a warmer basal colour and bears a distinctive canthal stripe that continues to the back of the head (v typically indistinctive and fades near ear). Resembles the Raukawa Gecko, but the Minimac Gecko is smaller, typically brighter in colouration and usually has a shorter snout. Resembles the Waitaha Gecko (p. 65), but the Minimac Gecko is smaller, generally has a shorter snout, and its rostral scale is separated from its nostrils (v in contact or near contact). **DISTRIBUTION** Coastal Whanganui-a-Tara/Wellington through to Whakatū/Nelson, Marlborough, Kaikōura and North Waitaha/Canterbury. **HABITS AND HABITAT** Nocturnal or cathemeral. Inhabits creviced rock outcrops, boulder beaches, rocky scrubland, scree and stony river terraces (from the coast to subalpine areas). Forages and shelters among dense vegetation, boulder banks, in crevices, or on or under rocks and logs. May bask cryptically. **CONSERVATION** Declining.

Kaikouras Gecko ▪ *Woodworthia* 'Kaikouras' ≤65mm SVL

DESCRIPTION Closely resembles its sister species, the Minimac Gecko (opposite); small and beautiful. Dorsal surface grey, olive-grey or brown, with pale markings (may bear speckles and orange markings, particularly on tail). Ventral surface pale brown or grey (uniform or speckled). Inside of mouth and tongue pink (tongue-tip may be grey). Resembles the Minimac Gecko, but the Kaikouras Gecko is typically found further inland, is more robust, and has more lamellae (10–12 v 9–11) and narrower toes. Resembles the Pygmy Gecko (p. 64), but the Kaikouras Gecko is larger. Resembles the Greywacke Gecko (p. 66), but the Kaikouras Gecko has a warmer basal colour and bears a distinctive dark canthal stripe that continues to the back of the head (v typically indistinctive and fades near ear). **DISTRIBUTION** Inland, eastern Marlborough and northern Kaikōura. **HABITS AND HABITAT** Nocturnal or cathemeral. Inhabits rocky scrubland, talus, rock outcrops and scree (from lowland to subalpine areas). Forages and takes shelter among dense vegetation, on rock surfaces, in crevices, or on or under rocks. May bask cryptically. **CONSERVATION** Declining.

Pygmy Gecko ■ *Woodworthia* 'Pygmy' ≤50mm SVL

DESCRIPTION Smallest gecko in Aotearoa/New Zealand. Dorsal surface olive-grey or grey-brown, with pale markings that resemble clouds (may bear speckles and dorsolateral stripes). Ventral surface pale grey (uniform or speckled). Resembles the Minimac Gecko (p. 62), but the Pygmy Gecko is smaller. Resembles the Southern Alps Gecko (p. 67) and Greywacke Gecko (p. 66), but the Pygmy Gecko is smaller (typically ≤50mm v ≥55mm SVL), has narrower toes and a blunter snout, and its rostral scale is excluded from the nostrils (v in contact or near contact).
DISTRIBUTION Inland Marlborough and North Waitaha/Canterbury. In the geographically separated Rangitata Valley-Ashburton Lakes population, individuals are much smaller (typically ≤42mm SVL).
HABITS AND HABITAT Nocturnal or cathemeral. Inhabits creviced rock outcrops, rocky scrubland, scree, talus and stony river terraces (from lowland to alpine areas). Forages and takes shelter among dense vegetation, scree, talus, on rock surfaces, in crevices, or on or under rocks. May bask cryptically. **CONSERVATION** Declining.

Waitaha Gecko ▪ *Woodworthia* cf. *brunnea* ≤80mm SVL

DESCRIPTION The most frequently encountered gecko in eastern Waitaha/Canterbury and very long lived (wild individuals have exceeded 50 years). Dorsal surface brown, grey or olive, with pale markings (may bear speckles, black spots and dorsolateral stripes). Ventral surface pale grey, brown or olive (uniform or spotted or speckled). Inside of mouth and tongue pink (tongue-tip may be grey). Resembles the Southern Alps Gecko (p. 67) and Greywacke Gecko (p. 66), but the Waitaha Gecko is browner in colour (v greyer in colour), has longer distal phalanges, often bears prominent black spots and is typically found at lower altitudes. Resembles the Minimac Gecko (p. 62) and Pygmy Gecko (opposite), but the Waitaha Gecko is larger. Resembles the Raukawa Gecko (p. 57), but the Waitaha Gecko has rostral scale in contact or near contact with nostrils (v in narrow contact or excluded). May hybridize with the Southern Alps Gecko in some inland areas. **DISTRIBUTION** Southern Marlborough through to mid-Canterbury, including Te Pātaka-o-Rākaihautū/Banks Peninsula. Present on predator-free Motunau Island. **HABITS AND HABITAT** Nocturnal or cathemeral. Inhabits scrubland, forest, creviced rock outcrops, rocky scrubland, boulder beaches, river terraces, scree, talus and boulderfield (from lowland to subalpine area). Forages and takes shelter on trees, among dense vegetation, scree, boulderfield, talus, on rock surfaces, in crevices, under loose bark, or on or under rocks. May bask cryptically. **CONSERVATION** Declining. Has been translocated to Pūtaringamotu/Riccarton Bush ecosanctuary.

Greywacke Gecko ■ *Woodworthia* 'Southern Alps Northern' ≤72mm SVL

DESCRIPTION Relatively abundant and brilliantly camouflaged. Dorsal surface grey, brown, olive or pinkish, with pale markings (may bear speckles). Ventral surface pale brown or grey (uniform or speckled). Inside of mouth and tongue pink (tongue-tip may be grey). Resembles the Minimac Gecko (p. 62) and Kaikouras Gecko (p. 63), but the Greywacke Gecko is more robust, found at higher altitudes, typically has 'V'-shaped markings on the head, has less prominent canthal stripe, and has rostral scale in contact or near contact with nostrils (v excluded). Resembles the Pygmy Gecko (p. 64), but the Greywacke Gecko is larger and its rostral scale is in contact or near contact with the nostrils (v excluded). Resembles the Waitaha Gecko (p. 65), but the Greywacke Gecko is greyer in colour (v browner in colour), has greenish or brown eyes (v typically yellow), and is typically found at higher altitudes. **DISTRIBUTION** Eastern Tiritiri o te Moana/Southern Alps in southern Marlborough to Rakaia River. **HABITS AND HABITAT** Nocturnal or cathemeral. Inhabits rocky scrubland, talus, boulderfield, scree, stony river terraces and creviced rock outcrops (predominantly Greywacke from lowland and montane valleys to alpine zone, ≤1,800m). Forages and takes shelter among dense vegetation, scree, boulderfield, talus, on rock surfaces, in crevices, or on or under rocks. May bask cryptically. **CONSERVATION** Declining.

Southern Alps Gecko ■ *Woodworthia* 'Southern Alps' ≤72mm SVL

DESCRIPTION Highly variable, brilliantly camouflaged and known to occupy extreme altitudes. Dorsal surface grey, brown, olive or pinkish, with pale markings (may bear thin mid-dorsal stripe and speckles). Ventral surface pale brown or grey (uniform or speckled). Inside of mouth and tongue pink (tongue-tip may be grey). Resembles the Kōrero Gecko (p. 71), but where these species overlap, the Southern Alps Gecko is smaller. Resembles the Kawarau Gecko (p. 70), but morphological differences are poorly understood; the Southern Alps Gecko typically has pale green eyes (v pale brown) and its toe-pads are often broadest in the middle (v broadest towards tip). Resembles the Waitaha Gecko (p. 65), but the Southern Alps Gecko is greyer in colour (v browner in colour), has greenish or brown eyes (v typically yellow) and is generally found at higher altitudes. Resembles the Pygmy Gecko (p. 64), but the Southern Alps Gecko is larger and its rostral scale is in contact, or near contact, with nostrils (v excluded). **DISTRIBUTION** Widespread in eastern Tiritiri o te Moana/Southern Alps, south of Rakaia River, to Wānaka in west and Naseby/Ida Range in east. **HABITS AND HABITAT** Nocturnal or cathemeral. Inhabits rocky scrubland, talus, boulderfield, scree, stony river terraces and creviced rock outcrops (from lowland and montane valleys to alpine areas, ≤1,900m). Forages and takes shelter among dense vegetation, scree, boulderfield, talus, on rock surfaces, in crevices, or on or under rocks. May bask cryptically. **CONSERVATION** Declining.

Raggedy Range Gecko ▪ *Woodworthia* 'Raggedy Range' ≤68mm SVL

DESCRIPTION Gracile, delicate and often has beautiful green-yellow eyes. Dorsal surface grey, brown or olive-brown, with thin, pale, raggedy markings (may bear speckles). Ventral surface pale grey or brown (uniform or speckled). Inside of mouth and tongue pink (tongue-tip may be grey). Resembles the Schist Gecko (opposite), but morphological differences are poorly understood; the Raggedy Range Gecko typically has smaller eyes, and its toe-pads are often broadest towards the tip (v broadest in the middle). **DISTRIBUTION** Raggedy Range north of Ida Burn. **HABITS AND HABITAT** Nocturnal or cathemeral. Inhabits rocky shrubland, rocky grassland and creviced rock outcrops (particularly foliated schist). Forages and takes shelter among dense vegetation and rock surfaces, in crevices, or on or under rocks. May bask cryptically. **CONSERVATION** Nationally Vulnerable. Currently thought to be range restricted but appears to be abundant in some areas.

Schist Gecko ■ *Woodworthia* 'Central Otago' ≤71mm SVL

DESCRIPTION Brilliantly camouflaged, with soft velvety skin and distinctive flattened appearance. Dorsal surface grey, brown or olive-brown, with pale markings (may bear speckles). Ventral surface pale grey or brown (uniform or speckled). Inside of mouth and tongue pink (tongue-tip may be grey). Resembles the Kawarau Gecko (p. 70), but morphological differences are poorly understood; the Schist Gecko often has yellow eyes (v never has yellow eyes), and has a narrow or no canthal stripe (v often has a broad canthal stripe). Resembles the Kōrero Gecko (p. 71), but where these species overlap the Schist Gecko is smaller (typically ≤70 mm v ≥70mm SVL), and its toe-pads are broadest in the middle (v broadest towards the end). Resembles the Raggedy Range Gecko (opposite), but morphological differences are poorly understood; the Schist Gecko typically has larger eyes, and its toe-pads are often broadest in the middle (v broadest towards tip). **DISTRIBUTION** East of Clutha Valley from southern Cairnmuir Range to Millers Flat, Beaumont northwards to Idaburn and along eastern edge of Maniototo Plain (present in southern Raggedy Range and Rough Ridge to Wedderburn). **HABITS AND HABITAT** Nocturnal or cathemeral. Inhabits rocky scrubland and creviced rock outcrops (particularly foliated schist). Forages and takes shelter among dense vegetation, on rock surfaces, in crevices, or on or under rocks. May bask cryptically. **CONSERVATION** Declining. Present in Mokomoko Dryland Sanctuary and has reached high densities in absence of mammalian predators.

Kawarau Gecko ■ *Woodworthia 'Cromwell'* ≤78mm SVL

DESCRIPTION Small and gracile at low elevations (typically ≤65mm SVL); larger and more robust at higher elevations (for example at Pisa Range or Mt Cardrona); highly variable. Dorsal surface grey or brown, with pale markings (may bear speckles and dorsolateral stripes). Ventral surface pale grey or brown (uniform or speckled). Inside of mouth and tongue pink (tongue-tip may be grey). Resembles the Schist Gecko (p. 69), but morphological differences are poorly understood; the Kawarau Gecko does not have yellow eyes (v may have yellow eyes) and often has a broad canthal stripe (v typically narrow or absent). Resembles the Mountain Beech Gecko (p. 72), but morphological differences are poorly understood; in the Kawarau Gecko toe-pads are often broadest in the middle (v broadest towards the end), and adult males only have two rows of precloacal pores extending on to legs (v three). Resembles the Southern Alps Gecko (p. 67), but morphological differences are poorly understood; the Kawarau Gecko typically has pale brown eyes (v pale green) and its toe-pads are often broadest in the middle (v broadest towards tip). **DISTRIBUTION** Clyde, and Mata-kānui/Dunstan Mountains to Wānaka and near Queenstown. Present on Mātakitaki/ Ruby Island in Lake Wānaka. **HABITS AND HABITAT** Nocturnal or cathemeral. Inhabits rocky scrubland, talus and creviced rock outcrops (from lowland to alpine areas, ≤1,300m). Forages and takes shelter among dense vegetation (including flax and cabbage trees on Ruby Island, Lake Wānaka), on rock surfaces, in crevices, or on or under rocks. May bask cryptically. **CONSERVATION** Declining.

Kōrero Gecko ■ *Woodworthia 'Otago/Southland Large' ≤95mm SVL*

DESCRIPTION Perhaps the largest species of *Woodworthia* (reaching largest size in alpine areas); robust and variable. Dorsal surface brown, grey or olive-grey. with paler markings (may bear speckles and dorsolateral stripes). Ventral surface pale grey or brown (uniform or speckled). Inside of mouth and tongue pink (tongue-tip may be grey). Resembles the Mountain Beech Gecko (p. 72), but adult male Kōrero Geckos only have two rows of precloacal pores extending on to legs (v three). Resembles the Southern Alps Gecko (p. 67), Schist Gecko (p. 69) and Kawarau Gecko (opposite), but where the Kōrero Gecko meets these species, it is generally larger, more robust and has broader toes. **DISTRIBUTION** Widespread in eastern Otago (including Ōtepoti/Dunedin) and Murihiku/Southland (south of the Waimea Plains) to eastern Fiordland. Present on several islands in Te Ara-a-Kiwa/Foveaux Strait. **HABITS AND HABITAT** Nocturnal or cathemeral. Inhabits forest, creviced rock outcrops, rocky scrubland and grassland, talus, boulderfield and scree (from lowland to alpine areas, ≤1,300m). Forages and takes shelter on trees, among dense vegetation, scree, boulderfield, talus, on rock surfaces, in crevices, under loose bark, or on or under rocks. May bask cryptically. **CONSERVATION** Declining. Present in several predator-free ecosanctuaries.

Muaūpoko/Otago Peninsula individual

Dunstan Mountains individual

Striped individual (Muaūpoko/Otago Peninsula)

Mountain Beech Gecko ■ *Woodworthia* 'Southwestern Large' ≤93mm SVL

DESCRIPTION Robust, beautiful and closely related to the Kōrero Gecko (p. 71). Dorsal surface pinkish-brown, grey-brown or olive-grey, with paler markings (may be speckled and bear longitudinal stripes). Ventral surface pale greyish (uniform or speckled). Inside of mouth and tongue pink (tongue-tip may be grey). Individuals from the forest typically smaller with brighter markings than those from alpine areas. Resembles the Kōrero Gecko and Kawarau Gecko (p. 70), but adult male Mountain Beech Geckos have three rows of precloacal pores extending on to legs (v two). Resembles the Southern Alps Gecko (p. 67), but the Mountain Beech Gecko is typically larger and has broader toes. **DISTRIBUTION** Eastern Fiordland (north of Motu-rau/Lake Manapouri) across to the Old Man Range and around Lake Wakatipu. **HABITS AND HABITAT** Nocturnal or cathemeral. Inhabits forest (especially beech), rocky scrubland and grassland, rocky lake shores, talus, boulderfield and scree (from the lowland to alpine and subalpine areas, ≤1,300m). Forages and takes shelter on trees, among dense vegetation, scree, boulderfield, talus, on rock surfaces, in crevices, under loose bark, or on or under rocks and logs. May bask cryptically. Native bat researchers have encountered it tens of metres up trees. **CONSERVATION** Declining.

Juvenile, Fiordland individual

Short-toed Gecko ■ *Woodworthia* 'Southern Mini' ≤65mm SVL

DESCRIPTION Petite, high-elevation relative of the North Island's Goldstripe Gecko (p. 59). Dorsal surface pale olive, olive-grey or olive-brown (may bear blotches, speckles and dorsolateral stripes). Ventral surface pale olive-grey (uniform or speckled). Inside of mouth and tongue pink (tongue-tip may be grey). Resembles the Mountain Beech Gecko (opposite), but the Short-toed Gecko has a warmer basal colour and is smaller (typically ≤65mm v ≥72mm SVL). **DISTRIBUTION** Southwestern Otago and northwestern Murihiku/Southland. **HABITS AND HABITAT** Nocturnal or cathemeral. Inhabits alpine and subalpine areas (600–1,700m) scree, talus, boulderfield, rocky herbfield, creviced rock outcrops and occasionally rocky scrubland or pasture. Forages and takes shelter among dense vegetation, boulderfield, talus, scree, on rock surfaces, in crevices, or on or under rocks. May bask cryptically. **CONSERVATION** Declining.

Delicate (Rainbow) Skink ■ *Lampropholis delicata* ≤55mm SVL

DESCRIPTION Aotearoa's/New Zealand's only established exotic skink; conspicuous and abundant. Dorsal surface uniform or finely speckled grey-brown or grey (may bear indistinct mid-dorsal stripe). Lateral surfaces bear darker band that is often edged with black and bordered by indistinct, thin pale stripes. Ventral surface pale grey, yellowish or white. Distinguished from all Aotearoa/New Zealand skinks by single frontoparietal scale on its head (v two in Aotearoa/New Zealand skinks). Most frequently confused with the Copper Skink (opposite), but the Delicate Skink has a single frontoparietal scale on its head (v two), lacks denticulate pattern on jaw and is typically more gracile. **DISTRIBUTION** Naturally widespread in Australia and Tasmania, but has been introduced to several other land masses, including Aotearoa/New Zealand. Now widespread in the North Island, and several small populations exist in the upper South Island. **HABITS AND HABITAT** Diurnal. Inhabits range of open, sunny habitats including urban areas (in coastal, lowland and montane areas). Basks, forages and takes shelter in or on dense vegetation or rocks. Annually lays 2–5 small white eggs. **CONSERVATION** Introduced and naturalized. Considered an 'Unwanted Organism' in the Biosecurity Act (1993). However, there is currently no robust evidence that indicates that it is outcompeting or preying on native lizards. Accordingly, killing these skinks is not advisable. Those doing so may inadvertently kill native skinks (misidentification often occurs). More research investigating its potential impact is warranted.

Copper Skink ▪ *Oligosoma aeneum* ≤76mm SVL

DESCRIPTION One of the most frequently encountered native lizards in the North Island; small and gorgeous. Dorsal surface brown or copper (uniform or flecked), often with thin, brown or copper dorsolateral stripes (which may be edged with black). Lateral surfaces resemble dorsal surface but are often more noticeably flecked. Ventral surface is yellow or cream (uniform or speckled), with pale grey throat and chin. Resembles the Ornate Skink (p. 79), but the Copper Skink typically has denticulate markings on its jaw (v usually absent), has a proportionately smaller ear-hole, lacks pale blotches on the dorsal surface and tail, lacks a pale tear-drop marking beneath the eye and is typically more gracile. Resembles the introduced Delicate (Rainbow) Skink (opposite), but the Copper Skink bears denticulate markings on the jaw and has two frontoparietal scales on its head (v one).

DISTRIBUTION Widespread in the North Island from southern Aupōuri Peninsula to Te Whanganui-a-Tara/Wellington. Present on many offshore islands. **HABITS AND HABITAT** Diurnal or crepuscular. Inhabits forest, scrubland, beaches, pasture and gardens. Cryptically basks, forages and takes shelter among vegetation, leaf litter, or on or under rocks and logs. **CONSERVATION** Declining. Present in several ecosanctuaries and on many predator-free islands.

Slight Skink ▪ *Oligosoma levidensum* ≤51mm SVL

DESCRIPTION The smallest native skink in Aotearoa/ New Zealand; thought to be secretive and rare. Dorsal surface light to dark brown (uniform or flecked), often with copper dorsolateral stripes (which may be edged with black). Lateral surfaces resemble dorsal surface. Ventral surface cream or yellow (uniform or speckled). Often has significantly reduced limbs. Resembles the Copper Skink (p. 75), but is not known to overlap geographically; the Slight Skink is smaller and often has smaller limbs. **DISTRIBUTION** Only known from northern Aupōuri Peninsula and Motuopao Island. **HABITS AND HABITAT** Diurnal or crepuscular. Inhabits native forest, scrubland and flaxland. May occupy invertebrate burrows. Forages and takes shelter among vegetation, leaf litter, or on or under rocks and logs. May bask cryptically. **CONSERVATION** Nationally Endangered. Has probably suffered from severe habitat loss.

Hardy's Skink ▪ *Oligosoma hardyi* ≤62mm SVL

DESCRIPTION An island-endemic relative of the Copper Skink (p. 75); gorgeous and small. Dorsal surface brown or golden-brown, with pale and dark flecks and pale brown or copper dorsolateral stripes. Lateral surfaces bear an indistinct dark brown band that often has pale and dark flecks. Ventral surface cream or yellow (uniform or speckled and may be flushed orange). Resembles the Aorangi Skink (p. 78) and Marbled Skink (p. 82), but Hardy's Skink typically lacks tear-drop marking beneath eye. **DISTRIBTION** Aorangi and Tawhiti Rahi in Poor Knights Islands. **HABITS AND HABITAT** Cathemeral or crepuscular. Inhabits native coastal forest, scrubland and flaxland. May occupy seabird burrows. Forages and takes shelter among vegetation, leaf litter, or on or under rocks and logs. May bask cryptically. **CONSERVATION** Naturally Uncommon.

Dylan van Winkel

Aorangi Skink ■ *Oligosoma roimata* ≤65mm SVL

DESCRIPTION An island-endemic relative of the Ornate Skink (opposite); robust and beautiful. Dorsal surface brown (uniform or flecked) often with golden dorsolateral stripes. Lateral surfaces resemble dorsal surface. Ventral surface white, cream or yellowish (uniform or speckled). Bears distinctive white tear-drop marking beneath eye. Resembles Hardy's Skink (p. 77), but the Aorangi Skink typically bears tear-drop marking beneath eye. **DISTIBUTION** Aorangi and Tawhiti Rahi in Poor Knights Islands. **HABITS AND HABITAT** Cathemeral or crepuscular. Inhabits native coastal forest, scrubland and flaxland. May occupy seabird burrows. Forages and takes shelter among vegetation, leaf litter, or on or under rocks and logs. May bask cryptically. **CONSERVATION** Naturally Uncommon.

Dylan van Winkel

Ornate Skink ■ *Oligosoma ornatum* ≤94mm SVL

DESCRIPTION Gorgeous, robust and secretive. Dorsal surface tan, crimson, brown or brown-black, often with pale blotches or flecks, which are particularly prominent on the tail. Lateral surfaces brown, grey-brown or orange-brown (often with vivid black, orange or yellow markings on sides of neck). Ventral surface yellowish, orange-red or cream (uniform or speckled). Bears distinctive white tear-drop marking beneath eye. Resembles the Copper Skink (p. 75) and Slight Skink (p. 76), but the Ornate Skink typically bears tear-drop marking beneath eye and is larger, more robust. Refer to the Hauraki Skink (p. 80), Coromandel Skink (p. 81), Whitaker's Skink (p. 83) and Robust Skink (p. 85) to see how the Ornate Skink differs. Resembles juvenile Chevron Skink (p. 87), but the Ornate Skink has a blunter snout, stockier body (with reduced limbs), and lacks distinctive chevron markings. **DISTRIBUTION** Widespread but patchy in the North Island from Aupōuri Peninsula to Te Whanganui-a-Tara/Wellington. Present on many offshore islands, including Manawatāwhi/Three Kings. **HABITS AND HABITAT** Cathemeral or crepuscular. Inhabits coastal and lowland native forest, scrubland and grassland. Forages and takes shelter among dense vegetation (often found in *Tradescantia*), leaf litter, or on or under rocks and logs. May bask cryptically. **CONSERVATION** Declining. Present in several ecosanctuaries and on offshore islands.

Hauraki Skink ▪ *Oligosoma townsi* ≤95mm SVL

DESCRIPTION Large, gorgeous and nocturnal. Dorsal surface light to dark brown, typically with pale and dark flecks. Lateral surfaces dark brown, black or grey, with pale cream or grey blotches. Ventral surface cream, grey or pale orange (uniform or speckled). Bears distinctive pale tear-drop marking beneath eye. Resembles the Ornate Skink (p. 79), but the Hauraki Skink is larger (typically ≥85mm v ≤84mm SVL) and has more prominent black colouration on the head and flanks. **DISTRIBUTION** Historically, widespread on the mainland North Island, but now restricted mostly to predator-free offshore islands in Marotere/Hen and Chicken Islands and the Mokohinau Islands. Present on Aotea/Great Barrier Island and Hauturu/Little Barrier Island. **HABITS AND HABITAT** Nocturnal or cathemeral. Inhabits coastal and lowland native forest, scrubland, boulder banks (particularly those with dense vines like *Muehlenbeckia*), and flaxland. May occupy seabird burrows. Forages and takes shelter among dense vegetation, leaf litter, or on or under rocks and logs. May bask cryptically. **CONSERVATION** Recovering. Highly vulnerable to mammalian predation and habitat modification.

Tim Harker

Coromandel Skink ▪ *Oligosoma pachysomaticum* ≤84mm SVL

DESCRIPTION Stunning, nocturnal and seldom seen. Dorsal surface light to dark brown, typically with pale and dark flecks. Lateral surfaces grey, brown or black, with pale cream or grey flecks. Ventral surface cream, grey or brown, usually with heavy flecks. Bears distinctive pale tear-drop marking beneath eye. Resembles Whitaker's Skink (p. 83), but the Coromandel Skink is smaller (typically ≤84mm v ≥85mm SVL), and has a cream, grey or brown belly (v orange-yellow). Resembles the Ornate Skink (p. 79), but the Coromandel Skink has more prominent black colouration on the head and flanks, a cream, grey, or brown belly (v typically yellowish), and is more robust. **DISTRIBUTION** Restricted to several predator-free islands in Mercury Islands, Aldermen Islands and Old Man Rock in Ohinau Islands. Historically, may have occupied the mainland. **HABITS AND HABITAT** Nocturnal or cathemeral. Inhabits coastal and lowland native forest and scrubland. May occupy seabird burrows. Forages and takes shelter among dense vegetation, leaf litter, or on or under rocks and logs. May bask cryptically. **CONSERVATION** Relict.

Tony Whitaker © The Museum of New Zealand Te Papa Tongarewa

Tony Whitaker © The Museum of New Zealand Te Papa Tongarewa

Marbled Skink ▪ *Oligosoma oliveri* ≤116mm SVL

DESCRIPTION Robust, beautiful and nocturnal. Dorsal surface light to dark brown, typically with pale and dark flecks. Lateral surfaces grey, brown or black, with pale cream or grey blotches. Ventral surface cream with dark blotches and markings. Bears distinctive pale tear-drop marking beneath eye. **DISTRIBUTION** Several islands and rock stacks in Poor Knights Islands. **HABITS AND HABITAT** Nocturnal or cathemeral. Inhabits coastal and lowland native forest and scrubland. May occupy seabird burrows. Forages and takes shelter among dense vegetation, leaf litter, or on or under rocks and logs. May bask cryptically. **CONSERVATION** Naturally Uncommon. Very vulnerable to mammalian predation and habitat modification.

Dylan van Winkel

Whitaker's Skink ■ *Oligosoma whitakeri* ≤101mm SVL

DESCRIPTION Only known from a few predator-free offshore islands; beautiful, nocturnal and rare. Dorsal surface yellow-brown, copper-brown or brown, typically with pale and dark flecks. Lateral surfaces dark brown, black, cream or yellow-brown, with pale cream or yellow blotches. Ventral surface orange or yellow (uniform or lightly speckled), with grey, dark brown or black throat and chin. Bears distinctive pale tear-drop marking beneath eye. Resembles the Coromandel Skink (p. 81), but Whitaker's Skink is larger (typically ≥85mm v ≤84mm) and bears orange-yellow belly (v cream, grey or brown). Resembles the Ornate Skink (p. 79), but Whitaker's Skink is larger (typically ≥85mm v ≤84mm), has more prominent black colouration on the head and flanks, and bears yellow flecks. **DISTRIBUTION** Historically, widespread on the mainland North Island but now restricted to predator-free islands within the Mercury Islands and Castle Island. Thought to be extinct at Pukerua Bay, its last mainland refuge. **HABITS AND HABITAT** Nocturnal or cathemeral. Inhabits coastal and lowland forest, scrubland and boulder banks. May occupy seabird burrows. Forages and takes shelter among dense vegetation, leaf litter, or on or under rocks and logs. May bask cryptically. **CONSERVATION** Nationally Endangered. Very vulnerable to mammalian predation and habitat modification. A breeding programme has been undertaken using the last remaining Pukerua Bay individuals, with the aim of reintroducing the species to other predator-free environments in the lower North Island.

McGregor's Skink ■ *Oligosoma macgregori* ≤119mm SVL

DESCRIPTION Extremely ferocious towards other lizards; large and rare. Dorsal surface light to dark brown, often with dark longitudinal streaks. Lateral surfaces brown or grey-brown, with prominent black markings and pale streaks (often flushed salmon). Ventral surface grey, cream, yellow or pinkish (may bear flecks). Bears distinctive pale tear-drop marking beneath eye. **DISTRIBUTION** Historically, widespread on the mainland North Island but now restricted to several predator-free offshore islands in Tai Tokerau/Northland, and on Te Mana-o-Kupe-ki-Aotearoa/Mana Island near Te Whanganui-a-Tara/Wellington.

HABITS AND HABITAT Nocturnal or crepuscular. Inhabits coastal and lowland native forest, rock shelves and flaxland. Forages and takes shelter among dense vegetation, leaf litter, or on or under rocks and logs. May bask cryptically. Long lived (known to exceed 50 years in captivity). **CONSERVATION** Recovering. Very vulnerable to mammalian predation and now only occupies <1 per cent of its former range. Has been translocated to two predator-free offshore islands in Northland. The eradication of mice from Mana Island has resulted in significant localized recovery.

Robust Skink ▪ *Oligosoma alani* ≤160mm SVL

DESCRIPTION Largest skink in Aotearoa/New Zealand; beautiful, nocturnal and bears striking large eyes. Dorsal surface brown, black-brown, olive-brown, yellow-brown or pink-brown, with pale cream or yellow blotches. Lateral surfaces grey, grey-brown or yellow-brown, with dark flecks, pale blotches and black markings above the shoulders (may be flushed bright orange or yellow along flanks). Coromandel individuals are markedly different and typically bear distinctive yellow tear-drop marking beneath eye, usually edged with black. Juveniles resemble the Ornate Skink (p. 79), but the Robust Skink has proportionately larger eyes, black irises (v red-orange), and typically bears prominent yellow blotches. **DISTRIBUTION** Historically, widespread on the mainland North Island, but now restricted to several offshore islands from Aupōuri Peninsula to Coromandel. **HABITS AND HABITAT** Nocturnal. Inhabits coastal and lowland native forest, flaxland and rocky scrubland. May occupy seabird burrows. Forages and takes shelter among dense vegetation, leaf litter, or on or under rocks and logs. May bask cryptically. **CONSERVATION** Recovering. Very vulnerable to mammalian predation. Has been translocated to several predator-free islands.

Northland individual

Falla's Skink ■ *Oligosoma fallai* ≤145mm SVL

DESCRIPTION One of Aotearoa's/New Zealand's largest skinks; very strong, agile and mobile. Dorsal surface tan, brown, olive-brown, golden-brown or pink-brown, often with pale or dark flecks and indistinct golden dorsolateral stripes (may bear dark mid-dorsal stripe). Lateral surfaces bear dark brown band that is often speckled. Ventral surface cream or yellowish (may be blotched or speckled) with grey chin and throat.

DISTRIBUTION Manawatāwhi/Three Kings Islands. **HABITS AND HABITAT** Cathemeral. Inhabits coastal forest, scrubland and fernland. May occupy seabird burrows. Basks, forages and takes shelter among dense vegetation, leaf litter, grasses, up trees, or on or under rocks and logs. Known to feed on fish regurgitated by seabirds and to climb several metres off the ground into trees. **CONSERVATION** Naturally Uncommon.

Chevron Skink ■ *Oligosoma homalonotum* ≤146mm SVL

DESCRIPTION One of Aotearoa's/New Zealand's most impressive reptiles; large, beautiful and elusive. Dorsal surface brown, yellow-brown, red-brown, grey-brown or copper with beautiful gold chevron markings (hence the Māori name niho taniwha, meaning 'teeth of the taniwha'). Lateral surfaces resemble dorsal surface. Ventral surface pale brown (uniform or lightly speckled). Bears distinctive denticulate markings along jaws, and tear-drop marking beneath eye.

DISTRIBUTION Aotea/Great Barrier Island and Hauturu/Little Barrier Island. Historically, widespread on mainland Tai Tokerau/Northland and may still exist in remote areas.

HABITS AND HABITAT Diurnal. Inhabits native forest (often near stream edges). Basks, forages and takes shelter among dense vegetation, debris dams, leaf litter, trees, ferns, clay banks, or on or under rocks and logs. Known to leap out of trees into streams and seek refuge underwater. **CONSERVATION** Nationally Vulnerable. Only known from a single mislabelled specimen and two records on Aotea/Great Barrier Island until the 1970s. Following this, more individuals were recorded, and their habitat use was studied extensively. Present on one predator-free island (Hauturu/Little Barrier Island), and intensive trapping is undertaken at Glenfern Sanctuary (on Aotea/Great Barrier Island) to protect a resident population. May greatly benefit from garden trapping and the reduction of mammalian predators on Aotea/Great Barrier Island.

Striped Skink ■ *Oligosoma striatum* ≤76mm SVL

DECSRIPTION Elegant, highly elusive and exceedingly arboreal. Dorsal surface mid to light brown, with distinctive broad cream dorsolateral stripes (may bear flecks). Lateral surfaces bear indistinct dark brown band. Ventral surface pale grey, brown or yellow. Resembles the Glossy Brown Skink (opposite) and Northern Grass Skink (p. 108), but the Striped Skink bears distinctive cream dorsolateral stripes. **DISTRIBUTION** North Island from Kaipara District to Waiariki/Bay of Plenty, Waikato to East Cape and down to Taranaki. Present on Aotea/Great Barrier Island and Hauturu/Little Barrier Island. May exist elsewhere. **HABITS AND HABITAT** Diurnal. Activity has also been observed at night during one captive-behaviour study. Inhabits native forest, rank pasture, and hardwood and pampas shelter belts. Basks, forages and takes shelter among dense vegetation, leaf litter, grasses, or on or under rotten logs or loose bark. Has occasionally been observed tens of metres off the ground, on tree trunks, or in large epiphytic platforms, where congregations of up to 40 individuals have been found. **CONSERVATION** Declining. Very cryptic, so conservation status is difficult to ascertain.

Dylan van Winkel

Glossy Brown Skink ■ *Oligosoma zelandicum* ≤75mm SVL

DESCRIPTION Sleek and relatively secretive. Dorsal surface brown or orangish (may bear pale and dark flecks). Lateral surfaces bear dark brown band that has crenulated or smooth edges. Ventral surface grey, cream or orange (uniform or lightly speckled). Resembles the Northern Grass Skink (p. 108) and Waiharakeke Grass Skink (p. 109), but the Glossy Brown Skink bears denticulate markings along jaw, and its belly is often orange (v dull yellowish or grey). Resembles the Copper Skink (p. 75) and Ornate Skink (p. 79), but the Glossy Brown Skink is more gracile, has a proportionately longer snout and bears a pale stripe on its forelimbs. **DISTRIBUTION** Southwestern North Island from Taranaki to southern Matau-a-Māui/Hawkes Bay to Te Whanganui-a-Tara/Wellington. South Island from Marlborough through to Tasman/Westland. Present on several predator-free islands in Marlborough Sounds and off the coast of Wellington/Kāpiti. **HABITS AND HABITAT** Diurnal. Inhabits native forest, scrubland, farmland, rock banks, grassland, wetland and gardens. Cryptically basks, forages and takes shelter among dense vegetation, leaf litter, or on or under rocks and logs. **CONSERVATION** Declining.

Kāpiti Coast individual

Kakerakau Skink ■ *Oligosoma kakerakau* ≤67mm SVL

DESCRIPTION Closely related to the Glossy Brown Skink (p. 89); gorgeous, and poorly understood. Dorsal surface brown, often with dark flecks and pale dorsolateral stripes (becoming indistinct past forelimb). Lateral surfaces bear dark brown band bordered by cream stripes from jaw to forelimb. Ventral surface brown or red-orange with dark speckles. Bears distinctive tear-drop marking beneath eye. Resembles the Moko Skink (opposite) and Striped Skink (p. 88), but the Kakerakau Skink typically has distinctive tear-drop marking beneath eye (v absent), distinctive broken mid-lateral stripe, and broken or indistinct dorsolateral stripes (v distinctive and continuous). Resembles the Northern Grass Skink (p. 108), but the Kakerakau Skink bears distinctive tear-drop marking beneath eye. **DISTRIBUTION** Initially discovered in Whirinaki Te Pua-a-Tāne Conservation Park and later at Te Whara/ Bream Head (Tai Tokerau/Northland) more than 300km away. May exist elsewhere. **HABITS AND HABITAT** Diurnal. Inhabits native forest and scrubland (often in forest clearings). May exist in forest canopy epiphytes. Basks, forages and takes shelter among dense vegetation, leaf litter, grasses, up trees, and on or under loose bark and rocks and logs. Known to climb trees (hence the Māori name, meaning 'to climb or scale trees'). **CONSERVATION** Nationally Critical. Extensive predator control and monitoring is being undertaken at Bream Head. Surveys have so far failed to detect it in Whirinaki Te Pua-a-Tāne Conservation Park.

Moko Skink ■ *Oligosoma moco* ≤81mm SVL

DESCRIPTION Distinctively striped, highly inquisitive and remarkably talented at seizing prey. Dorsal surface brown or copper-brown, typically with dark mid-dorsal stripe and cream or tan dorsolateral stripes. Lateral surfaces bear dark brown band bordered by clean-edged cream or tan stripes. Ventral surface uniform grey or cream. Intact tail very long and whip-like. Resembles the Kakerakau Skink (opposite), but the Moko Skink has distinctive, continuous dorsolateral stripes (v indistinct and broken), and does not bear tear-drop marking beneath eye. **DISTRIBUTION** Known from Waiariki/Bay of Plenty to Tai Tokerau/Northland. Present on multiple offshore islands. **HABITS AND HABITAT** Diurnal. Inhabits native forest (often in forest clearings), flaxland, scrubland, vineland, boulder beaches and grassland. Basks, forages and takes refuge among dense vegetation, leaf litter, grasses, up small trees, and on or under rocks and logs. **CONSERVATION** Relict. Relatively rare on mainland. Exists in one ecosanctuary and present on several offshore islands.

Egg-laying Skink ■ *Oligosoma suteri* ≤126mm SVL

DESCRIPTION The only native lizard in Aotearoa/New Zealand that lays eggs; beautiful and nocturnal. Dorsal surface golden-brown, cream, grey or black, with dark or golden flecks. Lateral surfaces resemble dorsal surface. Ventral surface grey, orange or pink (uniform or speckled). Resembles the Shore Skink (opposite) and Tātahi Skink (p. 94), but the Egg-laying Skink is more robust and has larger eyes. **DISTRIBUTION** East Coast of the North Island from Aupōuri Peninsula to Coromandel. Present on multiple offshore islands, including Manawatāwhi/ Three Kings Islands. **HABITS AND HABITAT** Nocturnal. Inhabits coastal areas such as shelly beaches, boulder beaches and littoral zone. Forages among dense vegetation, seaweed, near rock pools, or on or under rocks and logs. May bask cryptically. Known to dive into water and remain submerged for ≤20 minutes. **CONSERVATION** Relict. Only inhabits small fraction of its former distribution on mainland Aotearoa/New Zealand.

Shore Skink ■ *Oligosoma smithi* ≤82mm SVL

DESCRIPTION Gorgeous, sleek and a coastal obligate. Dorsal surface grey, cream, greenish, brown or black, usually with heavy speckling (may bear cream or golden dorsolateral stripes). Lateral surfaces black or bear brown lateral band that is often flecked. Ventral surface cream, yellow, pinkish, reddish, grey or black, with cream or white chin and throat (uniform or lightly speckled). Resembles the Egg-laying Skink (opposite), but the Shore Skink has smaller eyes, and is more slender. Resembles the Tātahi Skink (p. 94), but morphological differences are poorly understood. **DISTRIBUTION** East Coast of the North Island from Heretaunga/Hastings to Aupōuri Peninsula. Present on many offshore islands.

HABITS AND HABITAT Diurnal. Inhabits coastal areas such as shelly beaches, boulder beaches, duneland and littoral zone. Basks, forages and takes shelter among dense vegetation, seaweed, near rock pools, or on or under rocks and logs. Known to dive into rock pools to evade threats. **CONSERVATION** Declining. Present on several offshore islands.

Tātahi Skink ▪ *Oligosoma* aff. *smithi* 'Three Kings, Te Paki, Western Northland' ≤80mm SVL

DESCRIPTION Closely related to the Small-scaled Skink (opposite) and Shore Skink (p. 93); beautiful and intricately marked. Dorsal surface grey, sandy golden-brown, greenish or black, with heavy flecking (may bear golden dorsolateral stripes). Lateral surfaces bear dark brown band that is often flecked. Ventral surface cream, grey, pink, orange or yellow, with cream or grey chin and throat (uniform or speckled). Resembles the Egg-laying Skink (p. 92), but the Tātahi Skink has smaller eyes and is more slender. Resembles the Shore Skink, but morphological differences are poorly understood. **DISTRIBUTION** West Coast of Auckland from Muriwai to Muriwhenua/North Cape. Present on multiple offshore islands. Interestingly, a population also exists near Heretaunga/Hastings, which may have been inadvertently introduced by Māori during trading or migration many hundreds of years ago. **HABITS AND HABITAT** Diurnal. Inhabits coastal areas such as shelly beaches, boulder beaches, duneland, rank pasture and littoral zone. Basks, forages and takes shelter among dense vegetation, seaweed, near rock pools, or on or under rocks and logs. **CONSERVATION** Declining.

Small-scaled Skink ▪ *Oligosoma microlepis* ≤73mm SVL

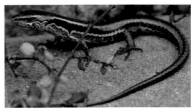

Juvenile

DESCRIPTION
Fascinating inland relative of the Tātahi Skink (opposite) and Shore Skink (p. 93). Probably evolved from Tātahi Skink ancestors when it became isolated as the coastline expanded outwards during the Pliocene. Dorsal surface brown or grey-brown, usually with flecks, mid-dorsal stripe and pale dorsolateral stripes. Lateral surfaces bear brown or grey-brown band bordered by pale stripes. Ventral surface cream or white. Bears distinctive pale tear-drop marking beneath eye. Resembles the Kupe Skink (p. 98) and Crenulate Skink (p. 96), but the Small-scaled Skink is smaller (typically ≤70mm v ≥75mm SVL) and bears distinctive tear-drop marking beneath eye. Resembles the Northern Grass Skink (p. 108), but the Small-scaled Skink bears distinctive tear-drop marking beneath eye. **DISTRIBUTION** Central North Island near Taupō, Rangitikei River, Ruahine Range and Taihape. Present on Motutaiko Island in Lake Taupō. **HABITS AND HABITAT** Diurnal. Inhabits open rocky habitats (especially pumice fields), such as scree, outcrops, cliffs, boulder banks, farmland and dense vegetation. Basks, forages and takes shelter among boulder banks, scree, dense vegetation, grasses, or on or under rocks and logs. **CONSERVATION** Nationally Vulnerable. One population exists on predator-free Motutaiko Island. However, elsewhere may be highly vulnerable and occupy very small, isolated pockets of habitat.

Crenulate Skink ■ *Oligosoma robinsoni* ≤90mm SVL

DESCRIPTION Northernmost member of the speckled skink complex; beautiful and robust. Dorsal surface brown with cream or gold dorsolateral stripes and light or dark speckles (may bear dark brown mid-dorsal stripe). Lateral surfaces bear dark brown band that typically has crenulated edges, is flecked with gold or cream, and is often bordered by cream or golden stripes. Ventral surface cream or yellow (uniform or speckled), with grey throat and chin. Resembles the Copper Skink (p. 75), but the Crenulate Skink is larger, lacks denticulate pattern on jaw, and bears conspicuous lateral band edged with cream or gold stripes (v lateral band absent or indistinct). **DISTRIBUTION** Waiariki/Bay of Plenty and Waikato through to Central Plateau. **HABITS AND HABITAT** Diurnal. Inhabits coastal and lowland forest edges, scrubland, grassland, pasture, fernland, boulder beaches and duneland. Basks, forages and takes shelter among dense vegetation, grasses, on sandy or rocky surfaces, or under rocks and logs. May bask cryptically. **CONSERVATION** Declining. Relatively rare on mainland but present on two predator-free islands – Mokoia Island (Lake Rotorua), and Moutohorā/Whale Island (Whakatāne Coast).

Hawke's Bay Skink ■ *Oligosoma auroraense* ≤100mm SVL

DESCRIPTION Closely resembles the Crenulate Skink (opposite); robust, stunning and rare. Dorsal surface mid to light brown, with cream or gold dorsolateral stripes and pale or dark speckles (may bear dark brown mid-dorsal stripe). Lateral surfaces bear dark brown band that typically has crenulated edges, and is flecked with gold or cream, and often bordered by cream or golden stripes. Ventral surface cream or yellow (uniform or speckled), with grey throat and chin. Resembles the Northern Spotted Skink (p. 134), but Hawke's Bay Skink is brown (v brown-green), and has a blunter snout and cream or yellow belly (v bright red-orange). **DISTRIBUTION** Central Hawke's Bay (for example Te Kauae-o-Māui/Cape Kidnappers). **HABITS AND HABITAT** Diurnal. Inhabits edges of coastal and lowland native forest, scrubland, grassland, pasture and duneland. Basks, forages and takes shelter among dense vegetation, grasses, on sandy or rocky surfaces, or under rocks and logs. May bask cryptically. **CONSERVATION** Nationally Endangered. Present in Cape Sanctuary. May greatly benefit from predator control and translocations.

Nick Harker

Kupe Skink ▪ *Oligosoma* aff. *infrapunctatum* 'Southern North Island' ≤80mm SVL

DESCRIPTION Named after the iconic Polynesian discoverer of Aotearoa/New Zealand, Kupe; handsome and thought to be very rare. Dorsal surface mid to light brown, with cream or gold dorsolateral stripes and pale or dark speckles (may bear dark brown mid-dorsal stripe). Lateral surfaces bear dark brown band that typically has crenulated edges, and is flecked with gold or cream, and often bordered by cream or golden stripes. Ventral surface cream or yellow (uniform or speckled), with grey throat and chin. Resembles the Northern Grass Skink (p. 108), but the Kupe Skink is more robust and heavily speckled. **DISTRIBUTION** Known from three disjunct populations – coastal Whanganui to Patea, Kaimanawa Forest Park and Wairarapa. May exist elsewhere. **HABITS AND HABITAT** Diurnal. Inhabits edges of coastal native forest, scrubland, grassland (including exotic grasses), pasture and duneland (in coastal, lowland, and possibly montane, subalpine and alpine areas). Basks, forages and takes shelter among dense vegetation, grasses, on sandy or rocky surfaces, or under rocks and logs. May bask cryptically. **CONSERVATION** Nationally Critical. Does not exist in any predator-free environments. May greatly benefit from predator control and translocations.

Newman's Speckled Skink ■ *Oligosoma newmani* ≤133mm SVL

DESCRIPTION Beautiful and highly variable; smaller on mainland (≤92mm SVL), much larger on Takapourewa/Stephen's Island (up to 133mm SVL). Dorsal surface brown with pale or dark speckles and indistinct pale brown-cream dorsolateral stripes (may bear dark mid-dorsal stripe). Lateral surfaces bear dark brown band that is usually notched (typically speckled and may be edged with black and bordered by pale cream stripes). Ventral surface bright yellow, yellowish, pinkish or salmon, with pale grey throat and chin (tail may be flushed pale blue). Refer to the Cobble Skink (p. 100), Kapitia Skink (p. 102), Hokitika Skink (p. 103), Alborn Skink (p. 101) and Boulenger's Speckled Skink (p. 104) to see how Newman's Speckled Skink differs. Resembles the Ōkārito Skink (p. 106), but morphological differences are poorly understood. **DISTRIBUTION** Whakatū/Nelson-Tasman down West Coast to Hokitika. May exist further south. Present on two islands in western Marlborough Sounds. **HABITS AND HABITAT** Diurnal. Inhabits edges of native forest, scrubland, grassland, pasture, fernland, boulder beaches, scree, rocky herbfield and duneland (from the coast to alpine areas). Basks, forages and takes shelter among dense vegetation, grasses, on sandy or rocky surfaces, or under rocks and logs. May bask cryptically. **CONSERVATION** Declining. Some populations have been severely impacted by habitat modification, mammalian predators and flooding. Has been translocated to Pākeka/Maud Island in Marlborough Sounds and Te Mana-o-Kupe-ki-Aotearoa/Mana Island near Te Whanganui-a-Tara/Wellington (the latter translocation may have been unsuccessful).

Stephen's Island individual

Greymouth individual

Cobble Skink ■ *Oligosoma* aff. *infrapunctatum* 'Cobble' ≤67mm SVL

DESCRIPTION Genetically unresolved and very rare. Dorsal surface mid to dark brown, often with pale or dark speckles (may bear darker mid-dorsal stripe). Lateral surfaces bear notched darker brown band that is typically speckled, and may be edged with black and bordered by pale brown or cream stripes. Ventral surface dull to bright yellow (uniform or speckled), with grey or brown throat and chin. Resembles Newman's Speckled Skink (p. 99), but morphological differences are poorly understood; the Cobble Skink is typically glossier and has larger eyes (distance from mouth to eye slightly less than eye height v approximately equal to eye height). **DISTRIBUTION** Only known from near Granity and Birchfield on the West Coast. **HABITS AND HABITAT** Diurnal. Inhabits coastal, deep cobble banks, with vegetation such as *Muehlenbeckia*. Cryptically basks, forages and takes shelter among cobblestones, dense vegetation, or on or under rocks and logs. **CONSERVATION** Nationally Critical. Was only known from a single tiny area near Granity and thought to have become extinct in the wild after a severe storm. However, in 2021 it was found at a new site south of Granity. A captive population is being managed and has successfully bred. Threatened by mammalian predators, coastal erosion, storms and land development.

James Reardon

Alborn Skink ▪ *Oligosoma albornense* ≤89mm SVL

DESCRIPTION Robust, cryptic and thought to be very rare. Dorsal surface light brown with pale or dark speckles and indistinct pale brown-cream dorsolateral stripes (may bear dark mid-dorsal stripe). Lateral surfaces bear notched dark brown band (typically speckled and may be edged with black and bordered by pale cream stripes). Ventral surface uniform ochre-yellow, with grey throat and chin. Resembles Newman's Speckled Skink (p. 99), but the Alborn Skink typically lacks belly speckles. **DISTRIBUTION** Only known from small area near Reefton on the West Coast. May exist elsewhere. **HABITS AND HABITAT** Diurnal. Known populations inhabit forest clearings, scrubland and pākihi wetland (in lowland and montane areas). Cryptically basks, forages and takes shelter among dense vegetation, or on or under rocks and logs. **CONSERVATION** Nationally Critical. Known from two tiny areas, one of which has disappeared since its discovery in the 1990s. Thought to be highly vulnerable to introduced mammals and habitat modification (particularly from shading out of habitat, fire and four-wheel drive vehicles).

James Reardon

Kapitia Skink ■ *Oligosoma salmo* ≤85mm SVL

DESCRIPTION Beautiful, rare and has a prehensile tail. Dorsal surface glossy brown, golden-brown or reddish-brown, often with pale or dark speckles. Lateral surfaces bear notched reddish-brown band that may be bordered by pale brown or golden-brown stripes. Ventral surface yellow (uniform or speckled), often with yellow or grey throat and chin. Resembles Newman's Speckled Skink (p. 99), but the Kapitia Skink is typically glossier and has more mid-body scale rows. Resembles the Alborn Skink (p. 101), but the Kapitia Skink typically has fewer ventral scales, fewer supraciliaries (five v ≥six), and generally has salmon and blue blotches on the underside of the tail-base (v lacks colourful blotches). **DISTRIBUTION** Only known from a small area near Hokitika (Chesterfield) on the West Coast. **HABITS AND HABITAT** Diurnal. Original habitat preferences unknown, but possibly coastal wind-swept forest and epiphytes (hence the prehensile tail). Now inhabits coastal exotic grassland near pasture and sand dunes. Very cryptically basks, forages and takes shelter among dense vegetation or under driftwood. Known to occupy mouse burrows. **CONSERVATION** Nationally Critical. Known from a single tiny area. Very vulnerable to habitat modification (particularly from farming) and has been impacted by extreme weather (coastal storms and flooding). A captive population is being managed and has successfully bred, and reintroductions have occurred within a specially built predator-proof fence constructed near the type locality.

Hokitika Skink ■ *Oligosoma* aff. *infrapunctatum* 'Hokitika' ≤85mm SVL

DESCRIPTION Poorly understood, only known from small number of individuals and thought to be very rare. Dorsal surface mid-brown or grey-brown, with pale or dark speckles (may bear dark mid-dorsal stripe and pale brown dorsolateral stripes). Lateral surfaces bear notched, dark brown band that is speckled and bordered by pale brown stripes. Ventral surface cream or yellow (uniform or speckled). Resembles Newman's Speckled Skink (p. 99) and Kapitia Skink (opposite), but morphological differences are very poorly understood; some Hokitika Skinks bear a discrete scale between the prefrontal scales (v absent).

DISTRIBUTION Only known from one area near Hokitika on the West Coast, and recently identified population near Cape Foulwind. **HABITS AND HABITAT** Poorly known. However, probably diurnal with similar habits to related species such as Newman's Speckled and Kapitia Skinks. **CONSERVATION** Nationally Critical. Only known from a few individuals, including two museum specimens. Probably threatened by mammalian predators, land development and severe storms.

Les Moran

Boulenger's Speckled Skink ■ *Oligosoma infrapunctatum* ≤80mm SVL

DESCRIPTION Mysterious relative of Newman's Speckled Skink (p. 99) that is only known from single museum specimen. Accordingly, variation is unknown. Dorsal surface brown with pale cream dorsolateral stripes and speckles. Lateral surfaces bear dark brown band bordered below by pale stripe. Ventral surface cream (uniform or speckled). Resembles Newman's Speckled Skink, Kapitia Skink (p. 102), Alborn Skink (p. 101), Kupe Skink (p. 98), Crenulate Skink (p. 96) and Hawke's Bay Skink (p. 97), but Boulenger's Speckled Skink has a discrete scale in between its prefrontal scales. Resembles the Hokitika Skink (p. 103), but Boulenger's Speckled Skink has eight supralabial scales (v seven). **DISTRIBUTION** Unknown. **HABITS AND HABITAT** Unknown. However, probably diurnal with similar habits to related species such as the Hokitika Skink and Newman's Speckled Skink. **CONSERVATION** Data Deficient. No extant populations known, and locality of holotype specimen unknown. May be very threatened and yet to be rediscovered, or has already become extinct, or simply represent previously unrecognized variation of another species.

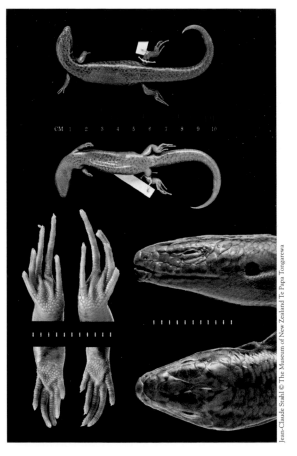

Jean-Claude Stahl © The Museum of New Zealand Te Papa Tongarewa

Westport Skink ▪ *Oligosoma* aff. *infrapunctatum* 'Westport' ≤75mm SVL

DESCRIPTION Genetically unresolved and only known from single museum specimen. Accordingly, variation is unknown. Dorsal surface brown with pale cream dorsolateral stripes and speckles. Lateral surfaces bear dark brown band bordered below by pale stripe. Ventral surface grey (uniform or lightly speckled). Resembles Newman's Speckled Skink (p. 99), Cobble Skink (p. 100), Kapitia Skink (p. 102) and Hokitika Skink (p. 103), but morphological differences are poorly understood. **DISTRIBUTION** Unknown. **HABITS AND HABITAT** Unknown. However, probably diurnal with similar habits to related species such as Newman's Speckled or Cobble Skinks, or Hawke's Bay Skink (p. 97). **CONSERVATION** Data Deficient. No extant populations are known. May be extremely threatened and yet to be rediscovered, or has already become extinct, or represent previously unrecognized variation of another species.

Jean-Claude Stahl © The Museum of New Zealand Te Papa Tongarewa

Ōkcrito Skink ▪ *Oligosoma aff. infrapunctatum* 'Ōkārito' ≤90mm SVL

DESCRIPTION Recognized as a distinct taxon in 2021; beautiful, cryptic and poorly understood. Dorsal surface light to dark brown with pale or dark speckles and pale brown, cream or golden dorsolateral stripes (may bear dark mid-dorsal stripe). Lateral surfaces bear notched dark brown band (typically speckled and may be edged with black and bordered by pale cream or golden stripes). Ventral surface uniform dull yellow or grey (may be lightly speckled) with grey throat and chin (tail may be flushed pale blue). Resembles Newman's Speckled Skink (p. 99), but morphological differences are poorly understood. **DISTRIBUTION** Only known from two small areas in Ōkārito on the West Coast. May exist elsewhere. **HABITS AND HABITAT** Poorly known. However, known to be diurnal, with similar habits to related species such as Newman's Speckled Skink. Inhabits forest clearings and edges, scrubland and pākihi wetland (in lowland and montane areas). Thought to cryptically bask, forage and take shelter among dense vegetation, or on or under rocks and logs. **CONSERVATION** Data Deficient.

Chathams Skink ■ *Oligosoma nigriplantare* ≤98mm SVL

DESCRIPTION The only lizard in Rēkohu/Chatham Island archipelago; robust and variable. Dorsal surface shades of brown, black, green or greyish, often with pale and dark speckles, and indistinct pale cream or brown dorsolateral stripes. Lateral surfaces typically bear notched dark brown band that may be edged with black and bordered by pale cream or brown stripes. Ventral surface uniform pale grey, brown or yellowish. **DISTRIBUTION** Rangiaotea/Pitt Island, its surrounding islands, and several isolated rock stacks including Rangitatahi/The Sisters and Tarakoikoia/The Pyramid. **HABITS AND HABITAT** Diurnal. Inhabits grassland, fernland, scrubland and rocky platforms. Basks, forages and takes shelter among dense vegetation, or on or under rocks and logs. Known to reach high densities on some islands. **CONSERVATION** Relict. Thought to be extinct on Rēkohu/Chatham Island but highly abundant on several predator-free islands nearby.

Edin Whitehead

Northern Grass Skink ■ *Oligosoma polychroma* ≤80mm SVL

DESCRIPTION Previously referred to as the Common Skink; abundant and widespread. Dorsal surface light to dark brown (rarely black or melanistic), with pale cream dorsolateral stripes (may be edged with darker stripes and bear prominent mid-dorsal stripe). Lateral surfaces bear dark brown band that has notched or smooth edges (may be bordered by pale cream stripes). Ventral surface uniform brown, grey or yellowish, with grey or white throat and chin. Currently indistinguishable from other grass skinks without the use of genetics. Resembles the Glossy Brown Skink (p. 89), but the Northern Grass Skink lacks denticulate markings along the jaw. Resembles Newman's Speckled Skink (p. 99), but the Northern Grass Skink is not as heavily speckled. **DISTRIBUTION** Widespread in the North Island from East Cape through to Taranaki, and Te Whanganui-a-Tara/Wellington. The South Island from Whakatū/Nelson-Tasman down West Coast to Hokitika. Present on several offshore islands. **HABITS AND HABITAT** Diurnal. Inhabits range of grassy and rocky environments (from the coast to subalpine and alpine areas). Basks, forages and takes shelter among dense vegetation, or on or under rocks and logs. **CONSERVATION** Not Threatened.

Waiharakeke Grass Skink ■ *Oligosoma* aff. *polychroma* Clade 2

≤80mm SVL

DESCRIPTION Delicate, abundant and often seen basking. Dorsal surface light to dark brown (rarely black or melanistic), with pale cream dorsolateral stripes that are often edged with darker stripes (may bear dark mid-dorsal stripe). Lateral surfaces bear dark brown band that has notched or smooth edges and is usually bordered by pale cream stripes. Ventral surface uniform brown, grey or yellowish, with grey or white throat and chin. Currently indistinguishable from other grass skinks without the use of genetics. Resembles the Glossy Brown Skink (p. 89), but the Waiharakeke Grass Skink lacks denticulate markings along jaw. Resembles Newman's Speckled Skink (p. 99), but the Waiharakeke Grass Skink is less heavily speckled. **DISTRIBUTION** Eastern Marlborough southwards to Wairau Valley and Kaikōura. Present on several islands in Marlborough Sounds. **HABITS AND HABITAT** Diurnal. Inhabits range of coastal and lowland grassy and rocky environments. Basks, forages and takes shelter among dense vegetation, under bark, or on or under rocks and logs. **CONSERVATION** Declining.

South Marlborough Grass Skink ■ *Oligosoma* aff. *polychroma*

Clade 3 ≤80mm SVL

DESCRIPTION Less frequently encountered than other grass skinks (largely due to low human habitation across its distribution); elegant and abundant. Dorsal surface light to dark brown (rarely black or melanistic), with pale cream dorsolateral stripes that are often edged with darker stripes (may bear dark mid-dorsal stripe). Lateral surfaces bear dark brown band that has notched or smooth edges and is usually bordered by pale cream stripes. Ventral surface uniform brown, grey or yellowish, with grey or white throat and chin. Currently indistinguishable from other grass skinks without the use of genetics. Resembles the Long-toed Skink (p. 131), but the South Marlborough Grass Skink is typically less heavily flecked, and has shorter toes and a much shorter intact tail. **DISTRIBUTION** Inland southern Marlborough, Seaward Kaikōura Range to northern Waitaha/Canterbury. **HABITS AND HABITAT** Diurnal. Inhabits range of grassy and rocky environments (from the coast to alpine areas). Basks, forages and takes shelter among dense vegetation, or on or under rocks and logs. **CONSERVATION** Declining.

Canterbury Grass Skink ■ *Oligosoma* aff. *polychroma* Clade 4 ≤85mm SVL

DESCRIPTION Delicate, variable and frequently seen sun basking. Dorsal surface light to dark brown (rarely black or melanistic), with pale cream dorsolateral stripes that are often edged with darker stripes (may bear dark mid-dorsal stripe). Lateral surfaces bear dark brown band that has notched or smooth edges and is usually bordered by pale cream stripes. Ventral surface brown, grey or yellowish, with grey or white throat and chin. Currently indistinguishable from other grass skinks without the use of genetics. Resembles Newman's Speckled Skink (p. 99), but the Canterbury Grass Skink is less heavily speckled. Resembles McCann's Skink (p. 114), but the Canterbury Grass Skink typically has notched dorsolateral/lateral stripes (v smooth edged in the Northern McCann's Skink), and is typically a warmer brown colour (v grey-brown). **DISTRIBUTION** North Waitaha/ Canterbury coast through inland Canterbury to West Coast near Hokitika and southwards to Ōkārito. May exist further south. Recently, a grass skink was found south of the Haast River, which may be this species. **HABITS AND HABITAT** Diurnal. Inhabits a range of grassy and rocky environments (from the coast to alpine). Basks, forages and takes shelter among dense vegetation, or on or under rocks and logs. **CONSERVATION** Declining.

Southern Grass Skink ■ *Oligosoma* aff. *polychroma* Clade 5 ≤80mm SVL

DESCRIPTION Highly variable, widespread and often seen basking. Two common and distinct morphs occur: a striped morph prevalent in Otago, Murihiku/Southland and parts of Waitaha/Canterbury; and a speckled morph prevalent in North Otago (usually at high elevations) and inland Canterbury. Dorsal surface light to dark brown (rarely black or melanistic), with pale cream dorsolateral stripes that are often edged with darker stripes (dark mid-dorsal stripe often present). Lateral surfaces bear dark brown band that has notched or smooth edges and is usually bordered by pale cream stripes. Ventral surface brown, grey or yellowish, with dull grey or white throat and chin. Dark brown or olive-green morph occurs in Awarua-Waituna Wetlands, Southland. Similar morphs occasionally seen elsewhere. Currently indistinguishable from other grass skinks without the use of genetics. Resembles McCann's Skink (p. 114), but the Southern Grass Skink is typically a warmer brown colour (v grey brown), and has a brown-yellowish belly with brown-grey chin (v pale grey-white belly and chin with speckles). Resembles the Herbfield Skink (p. 124), but the Southern Grass Skink lacks black markings and typically has smoother edged longitudinal stripes. Refer to the Nevis Skink (p. 115), Rockhopper Skink (p. 119), Burgan Skink (p. 116), Southern Skink (p. 127), Eyres Skink (p. 117), Cryptic Skink (p. 125), Pallid Skink (p. 123) and Oteake Skink (p. 122) to see how the Southern Grass Skink differs. **DISTRIBUTION** Eastern Canterbury, including Ōtautahi/Christchurch and Te Pātaka-o-Rākaihautū/Banks Peninsula to Otago and Southland. South-west from Aoraki/

Striped morph

Mt Cook to Motu-rau/Lake Manapouri. Population in Milford Sound may have been introduced. Present on several islands in Te Ara-a-Kiwa/Foveaux Strait and on mainland Rakiura/Stewart Island. **HABITS AND HABITAT** Diurnal. Inhabits range of grassy and rocky environments (from the coast to alpine areas). Basks, forages and takes shelter among dense vegetation, or on or under rocks and logs. **CONSERVATION** Declining. Present in several ecosanctuaries.

Speckled morph

Dark morph

McCann's Skink ■ *Oligosoma maccanni* ≤73mm SVL

DESCRIPTION One of the most frequently encountered skinks in the South Island; variable and widespread. Dorsal surface light brown, grey or grey-brown (rarely black or melanistic), typically with checkerboard-like markings and occasionally longitudinal stripes (especially in Waitaha/Canterbury and some of Murihiku/Southland). Lateral surfaces bear dark brown band that may be notched or smooth edged, and is typically bordered by pale cream longitudinal stripes. Ventral surface uniform pale white-grey or pale yellowish, with black speckles on throat and chin. Resembles the Southern Grass Skink (p. 112), but McCann's Skink is typically more grey-brown in colour (v warmer brown), and has pale white-grey belly (v brown-yellowish). Refer to the Nevis Skink (opposite), Eyres Skink (p. 117), Burgan Skink (p. 116), Rockhopper Skink (p. 119), Pallid Skink (p. 123), Oteake Skink (p. 122), Cryptic Skink (p. 125), Herbfield Skink (p. 124), White-bellied Skink (p. 133) and Roamatimati Skink (p. 132) to see how McCann's Skink differs.

DISTRIBUTION Inland Waitaha/Canterbury and Otago to Southland east of Main Divide. Population in Ōtepoti/Dunedin (on Muaūpoko/Otago Peninsula) may have been introduced, but a wild population was recently found on Scroggs Hill, slightly south of Dunedin. **HABITS AND HABITAT** Diurnal. Inhabits range of grassy and rocky environments (from lowland to alpine). Basks, forages and takes shelter among dense vegetation, scree, boulderfield, talus, or on or under rocks and logs. **CONSERVATION** Not Threatened.

Central Otago individual

Canterbury individual

Nevis Skink ■ *Oligosoma toka* ≤71mm SVL

DESCRIPTION Often found at extreme altitudes and may closely resemble the Eyres Skink (p. 117). Dorsal surface mid to dark brown (rarely black), often with dark mid-dorsal stripe and pale cream or yellowish dorsolateral stripes (may bear pale and dark flecks). Lateral surfaces bear dark brown band typically bordered by pale cream stripes. Ventral surface uniform mustard-yellow, with white throat and chin (may be speckled). Resembles the Eyres Skink, but the Nevis Skink typically has a mustard-yellow belly (v lemon-yellow). Resembles McCann's Skink (opposite) and the Southern Grass Skink (p. 112), but the Nevis Skink has three supraocular scales (v usually four) and mustard-yellow belly (v pale grey, and dull yellowish, respectively). Resembles the Rockhopper Skink (p. 119) and Pallid Skink (p. 123), but the Nevis Skink has three supraocular scales (v usually four). **DISTRIBUTION** Western and northern Otago from Nevis Valley and Tapuae-o-Uenuku/Hector Mountains, Old Woman Range, Mt Cardrona, Mt Alpha to Lindis Pass, Saint Bathans Range and Wether Range. **HABITS AND HABITAT** Diurnal. Inhabits rocky scrubland (particularly with *Dracophyllum*), talus, rocky tussockland, rocky river terraces and gold-mine tailings (from montane to alpine areas, 600–1,900m). Basks, forages and takes shelter among dense vegetation, talus, or on or under rocks. Known to curl tail over itself defensively. **CONSERVATION** Declining.

Burgan Skink ■ *Oligosoma burganae* ≤70mm SVL

DESCRIPTION Stout and gorgeous. Dorsal surface light or dark brown, typically with mixture of pale cream and black flecks, and pale cream or yellowish dorsolateral stripes (often bears notched dark brown mid-dorsal stripe). Lateral surfaces bear dark brown band that is typically notched and may be bordered by pale cream stripes. Ventral surface uniform grey or yellowish. Resembles the Southern Grass Skink (p. 112) and McCann's Skink (p. 114), but the Burgan Skink is usually more heavily flecked and has three supraocular scales (v usually four). **DISTRIBUTION** Inland Otago. Known from Rock and Pillar Range, Lammermoor Range, and near Lake Onslow. May exist elsewhere. **HABITS AND HABITAT** Diurnal. Inhabits herbfield (particularly with *Dracophyllum* and/or mountain daisies), woody or shrubby tussockland and cushion plant herbfield (from montane to alpine areas, 800–1,400m). May utilize insect burrows. Basks, forages and takes shelter among dense vegetation (particularly on the edges of shrubs) or on the ground. Known to curl tail over itself defensively. **CONSERVATION** Nationally Endangered. Previously considered Nationally Critical, but several new populations have been found. Highly vulnerable to habitat modification (particularly from fires and agriculture) and generally requires dense, woody vegetation to persist.

Eyres Skink ■ *Oligosoma repens* ≤62mm SVL

DESCRIPTION Gracile and vibrant. Dorsal surface yellow-brown or brown, typically with dark brown mid-dorsal stripe and pale yellowish dorsolateral stripes (may bear dark flecks). Lateral surfaces bear dark brown band, typically bordered by pale yellowish stripes. Ventral surface uniform lemon-yellow with white-grey throat (may be speckled). Resembles McCann's Skink (p. 114), but the Eyres Skink typically has a warm-brown dorsal surface (v grey-brown), lemon-yellow belly (v pale grey) and three supraocular scales (v usually four). Resembles the Southern Grass Skink (p. 112), but the Eyres Skink has a lemon-yellow belly (v dull yellowish) and three supraocular scales (v usually four). Resembles the Cryptic Skink (p. 125), but the Eyres Skink has three supraocular scales (v usually four). Resembles the Nevis Skink (p. 115), but the Eyres Skink has a lemon-yellow belly (v mustard-yellow). **DISTRIBUTION** Southwestern Otago, Murihiku/Southland, and northern and eastern Fiordland National Park. **HABITS AND HABITAT** Diurnal. Inhabits rocky scrubland, scree, talus and rocky herbfield (typically from montane and subalpine areas to the alpine zone). Basks, forages and takes shelter among dense vegetation, talus, scree, or on or under rocks. Known to curl tail over itself defensively. **CONSERVATION** Declining.

Mataura Skink ■ *Oligosoma* 'Mataura Range' ≤64 mm SVL

DESCRIPTION Recognized as a distinct taxon in 2021 following genetic analyses of a tissue sample collected several years before; very poorly understood. Dorsal surface yellow-brown, often with a thick, dark brown mid-dorsal stripe and pale yellowish or cream dorsolateral stripes (may bear dark flecks). Lateral surfaces bear a dark brown band typically bordered by pale yellowish or cream stripes. Ventral surface uniform yellowish with white-grey throat (may be speckled). Resembles the Eyres Skink (p. 117), but morphological differences are poorly understood. Resembles McCann's Skink (p. 114), but the Mataura Skink typically has a warm brown dorsal surface (v grey-brown) and three supraocular scales (v usually four). Resembles the Southern Grass Skink (p. 112) and Pallid Skink (p. 123), but the Mataura Skink has three supraocular scales (v usually four). **DISTRIBUTION** Southwestern Otago. Only known from Mataura Range and Mid Dome, but probably exists in other nearby mountain ranges. **HABITS AND HABITAT** Diurnal. Inhabits rocky scrubland, tussockland, scree, talus and rocky herbfield (subalpine to alpine areas). Basks, forages and takes shelter among dense vegetation (particularly speargrass), scree, or on or under rocks. **CONSERVATION** Data Deficient.

Rockhopper Skink ■ *Oligosoma* 'Rockhopper' ≤65mm SVL

DESCRIPTION Discovered in 2018; highly active and agile. Dorsal surface mid to dark brown, with dark and wide mid-dorsal stripe and smooth-edged pale cream dorsolateral stripes. Lateral surfaces bear dark brown band bordered by thin pale cream stripes. Ventral surface uniform yellowish with pale grey or yellowish throat. Resembles the Nevis Skink (p. 115), but the Rockhopper Skink typically has four supraocular scales (v three). Resembles McCann's Skink (p. 114) and the Southern Grass Skink (p. 112), but the Rockhopper Skink is typically more chocolate-brown in colour (v grey-brown or warm brown, respectively), with thin, bright longitudinal stripes (v wider, duller, rougher edged stripes). Resembles the Oteake Skink (p. 122), but the Rockhopper Skink lacks prominent dark spots or flecks on the dorsal surface. **DISTRIBUTION** North Otago, South Canterbury. Known from several mountain ranges in Oteake Conservation Park. May exist elsewhere. **HABITS AND HABITAT** Diurnal. Inhabits boulderfield (particularly vegetated edges or islands with *Dracophyllum*) and rocky herbfield (alpine areas, 1,300–1,650m). Basks, forages and takes shelter among dense vegetation, boulderfield, talus, or under rocks. Known to leap rapidly over rocks or off shrubs to evade threats, and to curl tail over itself defensively. **CONSERVATION** Declining.

Big Bay Skink ■ *Oligosoma* aff. *inconspicuum* 'Big Bay' ≤70mm SVL

DESCRIPTION Seldom seen and may comprise several unresolved taxa. Dorsal surface brown with dull black mid-dorsal stripe and dark flecks (may bear indistinct dull brown dorsolateral stripes). Lateral surfaces bear dark brown band that is often flecked, edged with black, and bordered by pale brown or cream stripes. Ventral surface copper-brown, yellow-brown or bright yellow (uniform or speckled), with a speckled pale grey to white throat. Tail keeled. Resembles the Mahogany Skink (opposite), but the Big Bay Skink has a blunter snout (v more pointed) and bold markings (v indistinct markings). Resembles the Taumaka Skink (p. 147), but the Big Bay Skink is smaller (typically ≤70mm v ≥75mm SVL), and has grey-green eyes (v black) and a keeled tail. Resembles the Okuru Skink (p. 129), but the Big Bay Skink has four supraocular scales (v three) and rough-edged longitudinal stripes (and lateral band), and is more heavily flecked. Resembles the Canterbury Grass Skink (p. 111), but the Big Bay Skink has a keeled tail, smaller ear-hole (v almost as large as eye), and bright yellow or copper belly with pale white throat (v dull yellowish). **DISTRIBUTION** Southern Westland from Big Bay to Cascade Plateau. May exist elsewhere. **HABITS AND HABITAT** Diurnal. Inhabits boulder beaches, scrubland and fernland (from lowland to subalpine areas). Basks, forages and takes shelter among dense vegetation, or on or under rocks. Known to climb high into small flowering shrubs. **CONSERVATION** Nationally Vulnerable.

Mahogany Skink ▪ *Oligosoma* aff. *inconspicuum* 'Mahogany' ≤70mm SVL

DESCRIPTION Astonishingly tolerant of harsh alpine environments; sleek and gracile. Dorsal surface warm chestnut to dark brown, often with minute pale and dark flecks, and dull mid-dorsal stripe (may bear thin, dull brown dorsolateral stripes). Lateral surfaces bear dark chestnut-brown band that is often flecked. Ventral surface speckled yellowish to bright yellow, with a black or grey throat (which may be speckled). Tail keeled. Resembles the Cryptic Skink (p. 125), but the Mahogany Skink is typically darker brown, and has a narrower snout, longer limbs and a keeled tail (keeled tail may be present in some unresolved western Cryptic Skink populations). Resembles the Big Bay Skink (opposite), but the Mahogany Skink has a more pointed snout and indistinct markings (v bold markings). Resembles the Awakōpaka Skink (p. 149), but the Mahogany Skink has a keeled tail, grey-green eyes (v dark brown-black), and is more gracile with longer limbs. **DISTRIBUTION** Known from Llawrenny Peaks and Transit Valley basin in Fiordland National Park. May exist on Mitre Peak and elsewhere. **HABITS AND HABITAT** Diurnal. Inhabits alpine creviced rock bluffs, vegetated ledges and rocky fellfield beneath cliffs. Occupies extreme high-altitude (>1,000m) habitats prone to avalanches, rock falls and intense weather. Basks, forages and takes shelter among dense vegetation, crevices, or on or under rocks. **CONSERVATION** Declining.

Carey Knox

Oteake Skink ▪ *Oligosoma* aff. *inconspicuum* 'Oteake' ≤70mm SVL

DESCRIPTION Seldom seen and quick to flee from potential threats. Dorsal surface chestnut-brown, often with a dark mid-dorsal stripe and numerous black flecks (may bear indistinct dull brown dorsolateral stripes). Lateral surfaces bear dark brown, rough-edged band that may have pale flecks and transitions to grey-brown below. Ventral surface grey-brown (uniform or speckled). Resembles the Southern Grass Skink (p. 112), but the Oteake Skink has a relatively small ear opening (v almost as large as eye), pale speckled throat (v

uniform), is more flecked, and the soles of its feet are black (v yellowish or brownish). Resembles McCann's Skink (p. 114), but the Oteake Skink has black soles of feet (v white or cream), and is more flecked and darker brown in colouration (v grey-brown). **DISTRIBTION** North Otago. Known from Oteake Conservation Park. An unresolved genetic relative has also been identified in the Solution Range, Westland. May exist elsewhere. **HABITS AND HABITAT** Diurnal. Inhabits vegetated boulderfield (particularly with snow totara) and fellfield (from alpine areas, 1,000–1,400m). Basks, forages and takes shelter among dense vegetation, boulderfield, talus, or on or under rocks. Known to climb over a metre off the ground into shrubs. **CONSERVATION** Nationally Vulnerable.

Mount Solution individual

North Otago individual

Pallid Skink ■ *Oligosoma aff. inconspicuum* 'Pallid' ≤70mm SVL

DESCRIPTION Predator naive at high elevations; closely resembles the Cryptic Skink (p. 125) and known to occupy extreme elevations. Dorsal surface dull brown or grey-brown, often with irregular dark spots, flecks and broken stripes (may bear dark mid-dorsal stripe and indistinct pale brown dorsolateral stripes). Lateral surfaces bear notched, dark brown band, which may be edged with black and bordered by pale brown-cream stripes. Ventral surface bright yellow or cream-grey and blotched, with a speckled, pale cream-grey throat and chin. Resembles the Cryptic Skink, but the Pallid Skink is duller (v glossier and bright), and typically has more extensive black markings on all surfaces. Pallid Skinks are also typically found at high elevations above the tree line (v usually lower elevations). Resembles the Eyres Skink (p. 117) and Nevis Skink (p. 115), but the

Pallid Skink usually has four supraocular scales (v three). Resembles McCann's Skink (p. 114), but the Pallid Skink typically has black markings on the dorsal surface (v no black markings), and a bright yellow or cream belly (v pale grey). **DISTRIBUTION** Murihiku/Southland and western Otago including Mt Cardrona, Tapuae o Uenuku/Hector Mountains, Coronet Peak, Mid Dome, and Mataura Range. May exist elsewhere. **HABITS AND HABITAT** Diurnal. Inhabits subalpine and alpine areas (≤1,825m) rocky tussockland, grassland and herbfield. Basks, forages and takes shelter among dense vegetation, boulderfield, talus, or on or under rocks. **CONSERVATION** Declining.

Herbfield Skink ■ *Oligosoma* aff. *inconspicuum* 'Herbfield' ≤85mm SVL

DESCRIPTION Beautiful, gracile and widespread. Dorsal surface light or dark brown, often with dark mid-dorsal stripe, black flecks and pale cream dorsolateral stripes. Lateral surfaces bear dark brown band that is often edged with black and bordered by pale cream stripes. Ventral surface bright yellow or yellowish (uniform or speckled), with pale cream-white throat. Resembles the Southern Grass Skink (p. 112), but the Herbfield Skink often has prominent black flecks (v none), smaller ear-hole and typically bears rougher edged longitudinal stripes (v relatively smooth edged). Resembles the Cryptic Skink (opposite), but the Herbfield Skink typically has brighter longitudinal stripes with smoother edges and greenish eyes (v brown).

DISTRIBUTION Eastern Otago to southern Murihiku/Southland.
HABITS AND HABITAT Diurnal. Inhabits coastal and lowland scrubland, wetland, duneland (where it occasionally occupies exotic ice plants) and rocky grassland. Basks, forages and takes shelter among dense vegetation, or on or under rocks and logs. **CONSERVATION** Declining.

Herbfield Skink (left) and Southern Grass Skink (right)

Cryptic Skink ■ *Oligosoma inconspicuum* ≤86mm SVL

DESCRIPTION Has several geographic forms that may be unresolved species or represent clinal variation; highly variable and widespread. Dorsal surface brown, chestnut-brown or reddish-brown, often with a dark mid-dorsal stripe, pale dorsolateral stripes and irregular pale and dark flecks. Lateral surfaces bear dark brown or reddish-brown notched band, often edged with black and bordered by pale stripes. Ventral surface grey-brown, bronze or bright yellow (uniform or speckled), often with a pale grey throat. Tail only keeled in unresolved western populations (for example in Humboldt Mountains and Wick Mountains). Refer to the Herbfield Skink (opposite), Pallid Skink (p. 123), Eyres Skink (p. 117) and Mahogany Skink (p. 121) to see how the Cryptic Skink differs. Resembles the Southern Grass Skink (p. 112), but the Cryptic Skink is typically darker reddish-brown

(v warmer brown), more heavily flecked and has rougher edged longitudinal stripes. Resembles McCann's Skink (p. 114), but the Cryptic Skink is darker reddish-brown (v grey-brown), with a grey-brown or yellowish ventral surface (v pale white-grey), and typically bears prominent dark flecks (v absent). **DISTRIBUTION** Western Murihiku/Southland and Fiordland (unresolved taxa) to western Otago. Present on several islands in western Te Ara-a-Kiwa/Foveaux Strait. **HABITS AND HABITAT** Diurnal. Inhabits range of rocky and vegetated habitats from lowlands to subalpine and alpine areas. Basks, forages and takes shelter among dense vegetation, boulderfield, talus, or on or under rocks and logs. **CONSERVATION** Declining.

Te Kākahu Skink ■ *Oligosoma tekakahu* ≤79mm SVL

DESCRIPTION Robust, sleek and very rare. Dorsal surface pale olive or chestnut-brown, with irregular black flecks (may bear indistinct cream dorsolateral stripes edged with black). Lateral surfaces bear dark brown band often bordered below by broken pale stripe (which may be edged with black). Ventral surface uniform bright yellow, often with a grey throat. **DISTRIBUTION** Only known from a small area on Kākahu-o-Tamatea/Chalky Island and the Green Islets, and a translocated population on Pukenui/Anchor Island in Fiordland National Park. May exist elsewhere. **HABITS AND HABITAT** Diurnal. Inhabits costal shrubland and herbfield. Basks, forages and takes shelter among dense vegetation. **CONSERVATION** Nationally Endangered. Was only known from a sliver of habitat on Kākahu-o-Tamatea/Chalky Island, but this has expanded to a wider area along the coastal slopes. A second population was found in the tiny Green Islets, 30km away, in 2018. Has been successfully translocated to Pukenui/Anchor Island.

Dylan van Winkel

Southern Skink ■ *Oligosoma notosaurus* ≤90mm SVL

DESCRIPTION Beautiful, highly variable and relatively abundant. Dorsal surface glossy, pale reddish-brown, chestnut-brown or dark brown, often with dark mid-dorsal stripe, and pale brown or cream dorsolateral stripes (may bear speckles). Lateral surfaces bear notched chocolate-brown band that is often edged with black and bordered by pale brown or cream stripes. Ventral surface grey-brown or bright yellow (uniform or lightly speckled), with grey chin and throat. Resembles the Southern Grass Skink (p. 112), but the Southern Skink is typically more robust and more heavily flecked on all surfaces, and its mid-dorsal stripe is usually broken and notched along the tail (v smooth edged). Resembles the Small-eared skink (p. 128), but the Southern Skink lacks a keeled tail, typically has a speckled ventral surface (v uniform), and has a narrower mid-dorsal stripe. **DISTRIBUTION** Rakiura/Stewart Island and surrounding islands. **HABITS AND HABITAT** Diurnal. Inhabits range of rocky and vegetated habitats from coastal duneland to subalpine areas. Basks, forages and takes shelter among dense vegetation, or on or under rocks and logs. **CONSERVATION** Declining.

Dylan van Winkel

Small-eared Skink ■ *Oligosoma stenotis* ≤75mm SVL

DESCRIPTION Unique, beautiful and seldom seen. Dorsal surface vibrant yellow-brown or greenish-brown, with a thick black mid-dorsal stripe (often edged with yellow), and pale cream or yellow dorsolateral stripes. Lateral surfaces bear smooth-edged, dark brown lateral band typically bordered by pale cream or yellow stripes. Ventral surface uniform light brown-yellow, bright yellow or yellow-green. Tail keeled. Resembles the Southern Grass Skink (p. 112) and Southern Skink (p. 127), but the Small-eared Skink has a prominent black mid-dorsal stripe, tiny ear opening and keeled tail. **DISTRIBUTION** Rakiura/Stewart Island from Hananui/Mt Anglem to southern Tin Range. **HABITS AND HABITAT** Diurnal. Inhabits subalpine rocky herbfield, tussockland and scrubland (480–980m). Basks, forages and takes shelter among dense vegetation, or on or under rocks. **CONSERVATION** Nationally Vulnerable.

Craig Stonyer

Okuru Skink ■ *Oligosoma* 'Okuru' ≤65mm SVL

DESCRIPTION Very mysterious and only known from a single individual. Accordingly, variation is unknown. Dorsal surface brown with black spots, an indistinct mid-dorsal stripe and pale cream dorsolateral stripes. Lateral surfaces bear brown band edged with black and bordered by pale cream stripes. Ventral surface uniform bronze or yellowish, with white throat. Tail keeled. Resembles the Southern Grass Skink (p. 112), but the Okuru Skink has three supraocular scales (v four) and a keeled tail. Resembles the Big Bay Skink (p. 120), but the Okuru Skink has three supraocular scales (v four) and a relatively smooth-edged lateral band (v rough edged). **DISTRIBUTION** Okuru, south of Haast (Westland). **HABITS AND HABITAT** Unknown. However, probably a diurnal species with similar habits to other West Coast skinks. **CONSERVATION** Data Deficient. No extant populations known. May be highly cryptic, extremely threatened and yet to be rediscovered or already extinct.

Tony Whitaker © The Museum of New Zealand Te Papa Tongarewa

Kahurangi Skink ■ *Oligosoma kahurangi* ≤76mm SVL

DESCRIPTION Discovered in 2017; gracile, highly active and has a very long intact tail. Dorsal surface brown, typically with thin dark mid-dorsal stripe and pale brown-cream dorsolateral stripes (which are typically bordered above by longitudinal brown stripes and may bear pale brown flecks). Lateral surfaces bear dark brown band that has rough edges and is bordered below by a pale cream or off-white stripe. Ventral surface uniform cream.
DISTRIBUTION Kahurangi National Park. May exist elsewhere.
HABITS AND HABITAT Diurnal. Inhabits alpine (1,500m) slate scree and rocky herbfield, tussockland. Basks, forages and takes shelter among dense vegetation, scree, boulderfield, talus, or on or under rocks.
CONSERVATION Nationally Critical. Initially only known from a single slate scree. However, surveys have now identified it in other locations.

Carey Knox

Long-toed Skink ■ *Oligosoma longipes* ≤80mm SVL

DESCRIPTION Highly active, alert and has a very long intact tail. Dorsal surface grey or brown-grey with indistinct, pale checkerboard markings (may bear indistinct pale dorsolateral stripes). Lateral surfaces bear notched dark brown band that may be bordered below by pale cream or off-white stripe. Ventral surface grey (uniform or speckled). Currently indistinguishable from the Roamatimati Skink (p. 132) without the use of genetics. Resembles the South Marlborough Grass Skink (p. 110), but the Long-toed Skink is greyer, has a more speckled dorsal surface and longer toes, and its intact tail is considerably longer than its body length (v equal to or slightly longer). **DISTRIBUTION** Inland South Marlborough. **HABITS AND HABITAT** Diurnal. Inhabits scree, talus, boulder banks, and rocky riverbeds and terraces (from montane to alpine areas). Basks, forages and takes shelter among dense vegetation, scree, boulderfield, talus, or on or under rocks. **CONSERVATION** Nationally Vulnerable.

Roamatimati Skink ▪ *Oligosoma* aff. *longipes* 'Southern' ≤80mm SVL

DESCRIPTION Closely resembles the Long-toed Skink (p. 131); highly active and has a very long intact tail. Dorsal surface grey or brown-grey with indistinct, pale checkerboard markings (may bear indistinct pale dorsolateral stripes). Lateral surfaces bear notched dark brown band that may be bordered below by pale cream or off-white stripe. Ventral surface grey (uniform or speckled). Currently indistinguishable from the Long-toed Skink without the use of genetics. Resembles McCann's Skink (p. 114), but the Roamatimati Skink has longer toes and its intact tail is considerably longer than its body length (v equal to or slightly longer). Resembles the White-bellied Skink (opposite), but the Roamatimati Skink has a notched lateral band (v smooth edged), typically bears checkerboard markings (v no markings or indistinct or broken longitudinal stripes) and lacks a mid-dorsal stripe (v mid-dorsal stripe often present). **DISTRIBUTION** Inland Waitaha/Canterbury to Te Manahuna/Mackenzie District. **HABITS AND HABITAT** Diurnal. Inhabits scree, talus, boulder banks and rocky riverbeds and terraces (from montane to alpine areas). Basks, forages and takes shelter among dense vegetation, scree, boulderfield, talus, or on or under rocks. **CONSERVATION** Declining.

White-bellied Skink ■ *Oligosoma hoparatea* ≤91mm SVL

DESCRIPTION Beautiful, highly alert and thought to be very rare. Dorsal surface brown, often with a dark mid-dorsal stripe (that is prominent towards the hindlimbs and tail-base), and pale brown-cream dorsolateral stripes. Lateral surfaces bear dark brown band bordered below by pale cream or off-white stripe. Ventral surface uniform pale cream or white. Resembles the Roamatimati Skink (opposite), but the White-bellied Skink has a smooth-edged lateral band (v notched), typically lacks dorsal markings or has indistinct or broken longitudinal stripes (v checkerboard markings), and often has a dark mid-dorsal stripe (v lacks mid-dorsal stripe). Resembles McCann's Skink (p. 114), but the White-bellied Skink is more robust, has longer toes and a more alert posture, and its intact tail is considerably longer than its body length (v equal to or slightly longer). **DISTRIBUTION** Inland mid-Waitaha/Canterbury. May exist elsewhere. **HABITS AND HABITAT** Diurnal. Inhabits alpine scree and talus. Basks, forages and takes shelter (particularly during a critical period in the morning), among dense vegetation, scree, boulderfield, talus, or on or under rocks. Known to bask with distinctive upright posture. **CONSERVATION** Nationally Critical. Only known from a few scree systems and thought to be highly impacted by mice.

Marieke Lettink

Northern Spotted Skink ■ *Oligosoma kokowai* ≤95mm SVL

DESCRIPTION Large, active and often bears brilliant iridescence. Dorsal surface brown-grey, brown or olive-green, with pale ocelli and flecks (may bear pale cream dorsolateral stripes). Lateral surfaces bear dark brown band that is often flecked (may be bordered below by pale cream stripe). Ventral surface uniform, bright red-orange, with white or grey throat. Resembles the Marlborough Spotted Skink (opposite), but the Northern Spotted Skink has a bright orange-red belly (v grey or pinkish). **DISTRIBUTION** North Island from Coastal Napier to Te Whanganui-a-Tara/Wellington. South Island from Whakatū/ Nelson to Saint Arnaud. Present on several offshore islands near Wellington and many in Marlborough Sounds. **HABITS AND HABITAT** Diurnal. Inhabits coastal and lowland grassland, duneland, scrubland, flaxland, fernland, edges of forest, boulder beaches and rocky areas. Basks, forages and takes shelter among dense vegetation, or on or under rocks and logs. **CONSERVATION** Relict. Very patchy distribution on the North Island mainland, but relatively abundant around Nelson. Present on several predator-free offshore islands. Present on predator-free Matiu/Somes Island, where it has reached high densities. Also translocated to Zealandia Te Māra a Tāne Ecosanctuary and Te Mana-o-Kupe-ki-Aotearoa/Mana Island. Napier population may greatly benefit from predator control and translocations.

Marlborough Spotted Skink ■ *Oligosoma elium* ≤89mm SVL

DESCRIPTION Large, obscure and beautiful. Dorsal surface brown-grey, brown or olive-green, with pale ocelli and flecks (often bears pale cream dorsolateral stripes). Lateral surfaces bear dark brown band that is flecked and often bordered below by pale cream stripe). Ventral surface grey or pinkish. Resembles the Northern Spotted Skink (opposite) and Canterbury Spotted Skink (p. 136), but the Marlborough Spotted Skink has more subdigital lamellae (≥24 v <24). **DISTRIBUTION** Marlborough and North Waitaha/ Canterbury from Ward to Hawarden. Present on predator-free Motunau Island. **HABITS AND HABITAT** Diurnal. Inhabits grassland, duneland, seabird burrows, boulder beaches, scrubland, tussockland, flaxland, edges of forest, rocky areas, scree, herbfield, fellfield, stony riverbeds and terraces (from the coast to alpine areas). Basks, forages and takes shelter among dense vegetation, scree, boulderfield, talus, or on or under rocks and logs. **CONSERVATION** Nationally Endangered. Seldom seen on mainland (where it has been impacted by mammalian predators and habitat modification) and may have been further impacted by the 2016 Kaikōura earthquake. Fortunately, it is relatively abundant on Motunau Island. Further research of mainland populations is warranted.

Canterbury Spotted Skink ■ *Oligosoma lineoocellatum* ≤110mm SVL

DESCRIPTION Large, striking and gorgeous. Dorsal surface brown-grey, brown or olive-green, with pale ocelli and flecks (may bear pale cream dorsolateral stripes). Lateral surfaces bear dark brown or brown-black band that is flecked (often bordered below by pale cream stripe). Ventral surface uniform grey, pinkish or suffused orange. Resembles the Marlborough Spotted Skink (p. 135) and Mackenzie Skink (opposite), but the Canterbury Spotted Skink typically has fewer subdigital lamellae (<24 v ≥24) and a more heavily marked tail. Dorsolateral stripes are also typically more pronounced on the Canterbury Spotted Skink compared to the Mackenzie Skink, which additionally does not bear denticulate markings on jaw. **DISTRIBUTION** Waitaha/Canterbury from Maukatere/Mt Grey to Rangitata River. Present on Te Pātaka-o-Rākaihautū/Banks Peninsula. May occur further south. **HABITS AND HABITAT** Diurnal. Inhabits grassland, duneland, boulder beaches, scrubland, tussockland, flaxland, edges of forest, rocky areas, scree, herbfield, fellfield, stony riverbeds and terraces (from the coast to alpine areas). Basks, forages and takes shelter among dense vegetation, scree, boulderfield, talus, or on or under rocks and logs. **CONSERVATION** Nationally Vulnerable. Becoming increasingly rare due to severe habitat modification and mammalian predators. May require habitat protection and extreme levels of predator suppression to thrive.

Mackenzie Skink ■ *Oligosoma prasinum* ≤94mm SVL

DESCRIPTION Robust, handsome and sparingly seen. Dorsal surface brown-grey, brown or olive-green, with pale ocelli and flecks (may bear pale cream dorsolateral stripes). Lateral surfaces bear dark brown or brown-black band that is often flecked and bordered below by pale cream stripe. Ventral surface uniform grey or pinkish. Resembles the Canterbury Spotted Skink (opposite), but the Mackenzie Skink typically has a duller brown dorsal surface with less distinctive dorsolateral stripes (v typically green, often with pronounced dorsolateral stripes), a less heavily marked tail and more subdigital lamellae (≥24 v <24). Resembles the Lakes Skink (p. 138) and Otago Green Skink (p. 139), but the Mackenzie Skink has two anterior subocular scales or three with a much smaller third scale (v three similarly sized anterior subocular scales) and typically lacks prominent markings on tail. **DISTRIBUTION** Te Manahuna/Mackenzie District and mid-Waitaha/Canterbury high country from Pukaki River south to Te Kiekie/Mt Somers. **HABITS AND HABITAT** Diurnal. Inhabits grassland, scrubland, tussockland, rocky areas, scree, herbfield, fellfield, stony riverbeds and terraces (from lowland to alpine areas, ≤1,500m). Basks, forages and takes shelter among dense vegetation, scree, boulderfield, talus, or on or under rocks and logs. **CONSERVATION** Nationally Vulnerable.

Lakes Skink ■ *Oligosoma* aff. *chloronoton* 'West Otago' ≤110mm SVL

DESCRIPTION Graceful and sleek member of the green skink complex. Dorsal surface brown-grey, brown or olive-green, with pale ocelli and flecks (may bear pale cream dorsolateral stripes). Lateral surfaces bear dark brown or brown-black band that is often flecked and bordered below by pale cream stripe. Ventral surface uniform pale grey (may be suffused with pink or orange). Resembles the Mackenzie Skink (p. 137), but the Lakes Skink has three anterior subocular scales (v two anterior subocular scales, or three with a much smaller third scale) and its tail markings are usually more pronounced. Resembles the Otago Green Skink (opposite), but morphological differences are poorly understood; the Lakes Skink typically has a longer snout (proportionately) and often has a duller brown dorsal surface (v typically green). Resembles the Southland Green Skink (p. 140), but this is more robust, with a shorter and blunter snout. **DISTRIBUBTION** Southern Te Manahuna/ Mackenzie District, western Otago and northwestern Murihiku/Southland from Pukaki River to Tākerehaka/Eyre Mountains and Tākitimu Mountains. **HABITS AND HABITAT** Diurnal. Inhabits grassland, scrubland, tussockland, rocky areas, scree, herbfield, fellfield, stony riverbeds, terraces and lake edges (from montane to alpine areas). Basks, forages and takes shelter among dense vegetation, scree, boulderfield, talus, or on or under rocks and logs. **CONSERVATION** Nationally Vulnerable.

Otago Green Skink ■ *Oligosoma* aff. *chloronoton* 'Eastern Otago' ≤110mm SVL

DESCRIPTION Large, energetic and often bears brilliant green colouration. Dorsal surface brown-grey, brown or olive-green, with pale ocelli and flecks (may bear pale cream dorsolateral stripes). Lateral surfaces bear black band often flecked and bordered below by pale cream stripe. Ventral surface pale grey (uniform or speckled). Resembles the Lakes Skink (opposite), but morphological differences are poorly understood; the Otago Green Skink typically has a shorter snout (proportionately) and often has a brighter green dorsal surface (v typically duller brown). Resembles the Southland Green Skink (p. 140), but the Otago Green Skink is less robust, with a more elongated snout. **DISTRIBUBTION** East of Whakatipu Waimāori/Lake Wakatipu through Central and North Otago and northern Murihiku/Southland. **HABITS AND HABITAT** Diurnal. Inhabits grassland, scrubland, tussockland, rocky areas, scree, herbfield, fellfield, stony riverbeds and terraces (from the coast to alpine areas). Basks, forages and takes shelter among dense vegetation, scree, boulderfield, talus, or on or under rocks and logs. Known to excavate burrows. **CONSERVATION** Declining. Relatively abundant in multiple high-elevation areas. Has disappeared from most lowland areas including Muaūpoko/Otago Peninsula, where it has probably been locally extinct since the mid-late 2000s. May exist on Wharekākahu Island near Cape Saunders. Has been translocated to Orokonui Ecosanctuary (Ōtepoti/Dunedin), and exists in one predator-free area near Macraes. Future translocations have also been planned.

Southland Green Skink ■ *Oligosoma chloronoton* ≤113mm SVL

DESCRIPTION Large, robust and exquisitely coloured. Dorsal surface brown-copper, brown or green, with striking pale ocelli and flecks (may bear pale or golden dorsolateral stripes). Lateral surfaces bear speckled black band that may be bordered below by a pale cream stripe. Ventral surface grey (uniform or speckled). Resembles the Otago Green Skink (p. 139) and Lakes Skink (p. 138), but the Southland Green Skink is more robust, with a shorter, blunter snout. **DISTRIBUTION** Catlins to Tiwai Peninsula and westwards to Te Anau. Present on Tihaka/Pig Island. May be present on some other islands near mainland in Te Ara-a-Kiwa/Foveaux Strait, for example Ruapuke Island. **HABITS AND HABITAT** Diurnal. Inhabits range of densely vegetated environments such as wetland, herbfield and scrubland (from the coast to montane areas). Basks, forages and takes shelter among dense vegetation, or on or under rocks and logs. **CONSERVATION** Nationally Critical. Severely impacted by habitat modification and mammalian predators. Status of island populations is uncertain. Would greatly benefit from predator control or translocations to predator-free environments and more survey effort to understand remaining populations. Recent wildfires may have impacted population numbers.

Stewart Island Green Skink ■ *Oligosoma* aff. *chloronoton*

'Stewart Island' ≤125mm SVL

DESCRIPTION Largest member of the green skink complex; robust and stunning. Dorsal surface brown or green, sometimes with dark flecks or black scales. On Whenua Hou/Codfish Island, often bears pale cream or pinkish dorsolateral stripes. Lateral surfaces bear black band that is flecked with pale cream-brown or gold markings. Ventral surface grey (uniform or speckled). **DISTRIBUTION** Rakiura/Stewart Island and outlying islands such as Whenua Hou/Codfish Island. **HABITS AND HABITAT** Diurnal. Inhabits coastal and lowland scrubland, grassland, forest edges, duneland, fernland and wetland. Basks, forages and takes shelter among dense vegetation, or on or under rocks and logs. **CONSERVATION** Nationally Vulnerable. Seldom seen on mainland Rakiura/Stewart Island and may now be very rare. Fortunately, this species is highly abundant on Whenua Hou/Codfish Island.

Whenua Hou individual

Port Pegasus individual

Tony Jewell

Grand Skink ■ *Oligosoma grande* ≤115mm SVL

DESCRIPTION Large, athletic and highly active. Dorsal surface vivid black and heavily flecked with gold, yellow or cream longitudinal streaks (these may form dorsolateral stripes). Lateral surfaces resemble dorsal surface. Ventral surface cream or grey (uniform or speckled). Resembles the Otago Skink (opposite), but the Grand Skink has longitudinal streaks or flecks on the dorsal surface (v prominent blotches), and is smaller and less robust. Resembles the Scree Skink (p. 145), but the Grand Skink lacks transverse bands (often present in Scree Skink), is typically darker in colouration with finer flecking, and does not inhabit large scree systems. **DISTRIBUTION** Western population near Lindis Pass and Lake Hāwea, eastern population near Middlemarch and Macraes Flat. **HABITS AND HABITAT** Diurnal. Inhabits schist rock tor systems and rocky shrubland or tussockland (from lowland to

subalpine areas). Basks, forages and takes shelter among dense vegetation, on rock surfaces, in crevices, or on or under rocks. Very fast and agile. Known to seize flies, cicadas and even bees from the air. **CONSERVATION** Nationally Endangered. Very vulnerable to mammalian predation and habitat modification. Present in Mokomoko Dryland Sanctuary and two predator-free areas near Macraes. Has greatly benefited from extensive conservation work that has included translocations and predator control.

Western form (juvenile)

Eastern form

Otago Skink ■ *Oligosoma otagense* ≤130mm SVL

DESCRIPTION Largest skink in the South Island; rare, striking and inquisitive. Dorsal surface vivid black with pale grey, dull greenish, yellowish, gold or golden-brown blotches (often bears pale brown or yellowish flecks). Lateral surfaces resemble dorsal surface (blotches are often smaller but may form large stripes). Ventral surface grey, off-white, cream or yellowish (uniform or blotched or speckled). Resembles the Grand Skink (opposite), but the Otago Skink has prominent large dorsal blotches (v longitudinal streaks or flecks) and is larger, more robust. Resembles the Scree Skink (p. 145), but the Otago Skink has prominent dorsal blotches (v small streaks or flecks, irregular blotches or transverse bands), is darker in colouration and does not inhabit large scree systems. **DISTRIBUTION** Western population near Lindis Pass and Lake Hāwea, eastern population near Middlemarch and Macraes Flat. **HABITS AND HABITAT** Diurnal. Inhabits schist rock tor systems (from lowland to subalpine areas). Basks, forages and takes shelter among dense vegetation, on rock surfaces, in crevices, or on or under rocks. Highly social and often basks in groups. **CONSERVATION** Nationally Endangered. Very vulnerable to mammalian predation and habitat modification. Thought to occupy <8 per cent of its historical range. Present in Mokomoko Dryland Sanctuary and a predator-free area near Macraes. Has greatly benefited from extensive conservation work that has included translocations and predator control.

Western form

Eastern form

Marlborough Scree Skink ■ *Oligosoma* aff. *waimatense* 'Marlborough'
≤114mm SVL

DESCRIPTION Large, beautiful and seldom seen. Dorsal surface cream-yellowish, golden-tan or greyish, often with a greenish sheen, black transverse bands and thin longitudinal streak (may bear indistinct pale dorsolateral stripes where black markings are absent). Lateral surfaces resemble dorsal surface but may be paler and become uniform grey near lower portion. Ventral surface uniform grey (belly may be flushed pink). **DISTRIBUTION** Marlborough from the Wairau River to the Clarence River and Kaikōura Ranges. **HABITS AND HABITAT** Diurnal. Inhabits creviced rock bluffs, alluvial fans, rocky riverbeds and terraces, boulderfield and scree (from lowland to alpine areas, 1,800m). Basks, forages and takes shelter among dense vegetation, scree, boulderfield, talus, in crevices, or on or under rocks. **CONSERVATION** Nationally Endangered.

Carey Knox

Scree Skink ■ *Oligosoma waimatense* ≤114mm SVL

DESCRIPTION Large, active and highly mobile. Genetic analyses indicate that the Otago population has hybridized with the Otago Skink (p. 143). Dorsal surface typically drab grey or bright cream-yellow (in Otago form), often with greenish sheen, black transverse bands and dense black flecks (may bear indistinct pale dorsolateral stripes where black markings are absent). Lateral surfaces resemble dorsal surface but may become uniform grey near lower portion and black bands may be absent (in Canterbury form). Ventral surface uniform pale grey (belly may be flushed pale orange). Resembles the Alpine Rock Skink (p. 146), but the Scree Skink is more grey-cream (v black with green-yellow accents), more robust, and has a proportionately shorter and blunter snout, more mid-body scale rows (50–68 v 44), and more lamellae (30–34 v 24–25). Resembles the Roamatimati Skink (p. 132), but the Scree Skink is larger and more robust (≤75mm v >75mm SVL), greyer (v browner), and lacks lateral band (v has notched brown lateral band). **DISTRIBUTION** South to mid-Waitaha/Canterbury and Waitaki to Oteake Conservation Park (North Otago). **HABITS AND HABITAT** Diurnal. Inhabits creviced rock bluffs, alluvial fans, rocky riverbeds and terraces, boulderfield and scree (from lowland to alpine areas, ≤1,500m). Basks, forages and takes shelter among dense vegetation, scree, boulderfield, talus, in crevices, or on or under rocks. **CONSERVATION** Nationally Vulnerable.

Canterbury individual

Otago individual

Alpine Rock Skink ■ *Oligosoma* aff. *waimatense* 'Alpine Rock' ≤89mm SVL

DESCRIPTION Discovered in 2018; highly alert and graceful. Dorsal surface black to dark brown, with small, irregular yellowish or blue-green gold flecks. Lateral surfaces resemble dorsal surface. Ventral surface uniform green-grey or cream, often with green or blue sheen. Resembles the Scree Skink (p. 145), but the Alpine Rock Skink is darker and more slender, and has a proportionately narrower snout, fewer mid-body scale rows (44 v 50–68), and fewer lamellae (24–25 v 30–34). **DISTRIBUTION** North Otago (Oteake Conservation Park) to Te Manahuna/ Mackenzie District. **HABITS AND HABITAT** Diurnal. Inhabits boulderfield, scree and talus (from subalpine to alpine areas, 1,100–1,650m). Basks, forages and takes shelter among dense vegetation, scree, boulderfield, talus, in crevices, or on or under rocks. Known to be very quick, alert, cautious and highly mobile. Also known to co-exist with Scree Skink. **CONSERVATION** Nationally Vulnerable. Extensive surveys have identified the species across several mountain ranges and more populations may be discovered.

Taumaka Skink ■ *Oligosoma taumakae* ≤96mm SVL

DESCRIPTION Robust, rare and inquisitive. Dorsal surface brown, grey-brown or olive-brown, with dark flecks (often bears pale cream dorsolateral stripes). Lateral surfaces bear dark brown band and often heavily flecked with pale markings (often bordered below by pale grey-cream stripe). Ventral surface pale yellow and speckled. **DISTRIBUTION** Open Bay Islands and Barn Islands. May exist on adjacent mainland. **HABITS AND HABITAT** Diurnal. Inhabits coastal forest, scrubland, grassland and rocky areas. Basks, forages and takes shelter among dense vegetation, leaf litter, or on or under rocks and logs. Known to form large aggregations when basking. **CONSERVATION** Nationally Endangered. Highly vulnerable to predators. Weka co-occur with this species in Open Bay Islands, and it may be highly beneficial to investigate their potential impact.

Marieke Lettink

Fiordland Skink ■ *Oligosoma acrinasum* ≤88mm SVL

DESCRIPTION Remarkably tolerant of harsh coastal environments; sleek and highly social. Dorsal surface glossy black or dark brown, often with yellowish, greenish or brown flecks or speckles (which may form thin dorsolateral stripes). Lateral surfaces speckled and often bear dark brown or black band. Ventral surface green-grey (speckled or blotched). **DISTRIBUTION** Southwestern Fiordland National Park. Present on several offshore islands and islets. **HABITS AND HABITAT** Diurnal. Inhabits creviced rock outcrops and boulder beaches on Fiordland's frigid southwestern coastline. Occupies extreme coastal habitats, which are exposed to intense weather and often inundated by violent waves. Basks, forages and takes shelter among dense vegetation, on rocky surfaces, in crevices, or on or under rocks and logs. Known to dive into rock pools to evade threats. Large aggregations of these skinks are often seen, as they bask communally. Also known to disperse between islets. **CONSERVATION** Nationally Vulnerable. Surveys have identified this species on several predator-free islands and islets, and rocky shores. Highly threatened by predators and only persists where these are absent.

Dylan van Winkel

Jo Monks

Awakōpaka Skink ■ *Oligosoma awakopaka* ≤77mm SVL

DESCRIPTION Highly unique, elusive and thought to be extremely rare. Dorsal surface glossy brown-yellow or brown, with black flecks or speckles (may bear faint pale yellow-brown dorsolateral stripe). Lateral surfaces resemble dorsal surface, but are often more heavily flecked with black (may bear an irregular dark band and pale yellow spots). Ventral surface bright yellow or grey-yellow, with speckles and grey or grey-brown throat. **DISTRIBUTION** Only known from Darran Mountains (Fiordland National Park). May exist elsewhere, but much of its potential habitat is very difficult to access and survey. **HABITS AND HABITAT** Diurnal. Inhabits rocky herbfield or fellfield beneath cliffs. Occupies extreme alpine (>1,000m) habitats prone to avalanches and rock falls (hence the Māori name meaning 'skink that lives in the footprints of mighty glaciers'). Thought to cryptically bask, forage and take shelter among dense vegetation, in crevices, or on or under rocks. **CONSERVATION** Nationally Critical. Very few have ever been found. Known from single tiny area of less than 2ha. Several surveys further afield have failed to locate more populations. However, it is incredibly cryptic and may be awaiting discovery.

Barrier Skink ■ *Oligosoma judgei* ≤97mm SVL

DESCRIPTION One of Aotearoa's/New Zealand's most extreme alpine reptiles; large and highly mobile. Dorsal surface black, with vivid green, cream or yellow-golden flecks (often bears yellow-golden dorsolateral stripes that extend from the nostrils down the tail). Lateral surfaces bear broad black band with vivid green, yellow-golden or cream blotches. Ventral surface white or cream and speckled. Resembles the closely related Sinbad Skink (opposite), but the Barrier Skink is typically more robust, duller (with less green), and has a white-cream belly (v flushed orange), more ventral scale rows (90–97 v 78–88) and more lamellae (24–25 v 20–23). **DISTRIBUTION** Only known from Fiordland National Park and Tākitimu Mountains. May exist elsewhere. **HABITS AND HABITAT** Diurnal. Inhabits alpine creviced rock bluffs, scree, boulderfield, vegetated ledges and rocky fellfield or herbfield. Occupies extreme high-altitude (1,030–1,870m) habitats prone to avalanches, rock falls and intense weather. Basks, forages and takes shelter among dense vegetation, in crevices, on rocky surfaces, or on or under rocks. Some high-altitude populations are extremely naive and may rarely encounter predators. **CONSERVATION** Nationally Endangered. Highly vulnerable to predators, which are becoming more prevalent in its habitats (this may be exacerbated by climate change). Only known from five general locations.

Tony Jewell

Sinbad Skink ▪ *Oligosoma pikitanga* ≤91mm SVL

DESCRIPTION Astonishingly tolerant of harsh alpine environments; exquisite and rare. Dorsal surface glossy black with brilliant green, olive or olive-brown blotches or flecks (often bears black mid-dorsal stripe and irregular copper or pink gold colouration on tail). Lateral surfaces typically bear black band that runs from the nostrils to the tail and has rough edges (often scored with salmon or pink-gold blotches). Ventral surface uniform orange-red, with pale grey or pinkish chin and throat. Resembles the Barrier Skink (opposite), but the Sinbad Skink is typically greener, and has an orange-flushed belly (v white-cream), fewer ventral scale rows (78–88 v 90–97), and fewer lamellae (20–23 v 24–25). **DISTRIBUTION** Only known from Sinbad Gully (Fiordland National Park). May exist elsewhere, but much of its potential habitat is very difficult to access and survey. **HABITS AND HABITAT** Diurnal. Inhabits alpine creviced rock bluffs, vegetated ledges and rocky fellfield beneath cliffs. Occupies extreme habitats prone to avalanches, rock falls and intense weather (>1,000m). Basks, forages and takes shelter among dense vegetation, in crevices, on rocky surfaces, or on or under rocks. **CONSERVATION** Nationally Endangered. Highly vulnerable to predators. Monitoring has indicated that population numbers are stable. However, robust population estimates are difficult to produce due to the inaccessible nature of its habitat. Identifying the species elsewhere would be of immense conservation value.

Carey Knox

Hochstetter's Frog ▪ *Leiopelma hochstetteri* ≤47mm (females), ≤38mm (males) SVL

DESCRIPION The only native frog with a free-swimming larval stage; brilliantly camouflaged and relatively widespread. Dorsal surface light to dark brown, reddish-brown, green-brown or yellow (rarely) often with dark blotches and bands (particularly on hindlegs and forelimbs). Lateral surfaces resemble dorsal surface. Ventral surface pale brown or yellow-brown. Skin covered with tubercules and appears very warty. Males considerably smaller than females and possess more robust forelimbs. Resembles Archey's Frog (opposite), but Hochstetter's Frog is more robust and has more granular (warty) skin and semi-webbed hind-toes (v unwebbed). **DISTRIBUTION** Historically, widespread in the North Island and north-west South Island. Now has fragmented populations from Waipū (Tai Tokerau/Northland) to Waiariki/Bay of Plenty, Waikato (Whareorino and Maungatautari) and East Cape. Present on Aotea/ Great Barrier Island.

HABITS AND HABITAT Nocturnal. Inhabits seepages and streams in native forest and occasionally exotic plantation or farmland (from the coast to montane areas). Forages and takes shelter in and around streams, dense vegetation and leaf litter, in crevices, up plants, or on or under damp logs and rocks. Does not produce a mating call. May use visual or chemical cues for reproductive behaviour. **CONSERVATION** Declining. Present in Sanctuary Mountain Maungatautari ecosanctuary.

Archey's Frog ■ *Leiopelma archeyi* ≤40mm (females), ≤30mm (males) SVL

DESCRIPTION Smallest frog in Aotearoa/New Zealand; strikingly beautiful and rare. Dorsal surface typically light to dark brown, green-brown or green, often with dark blotches, speckles and bands (particularly on hindlegs and forelimbs). May bear bluish accents. Also bears conspicuous lumps (glandular ridges) on dorsolateral surfaces. Lateral surfaces often bear large black blotches and may be flushed pinkish or orange. Ventral surface brown or black, and heavily blotched. **DISTRIBUTION** Historically, widespread in the North Island. Now only known from Te Tara-o-te-Ika a Māui/ Coromandel Peninsula, Whareorino Forest (near Te Kuiti), and a translocated population at Pureora Forest Park. **HABITS AND HABITAT** Nocturnal (occasionally emerges on damp days). Inhabits damp native forest, particularly high-elevation cloud forest (from the coast to montane areas). Forages and takes shelter among dense vegetation, leaf litter, on

or under damp logs and rocks, or up trees and other plants. Does not produce a mating call. May use visual or chemical cues for reproductive behaviour. **CONSERVATION** Declining. Appears to have benefited from extensive conservation work that includes translocations, monitoring and rat control. Does not occur in any wild, predator-free environments.

Male guarding eggs

Euan Brook

Hamilton's Frog ■ *Leiopelma hamiltoni* ≤52mm (females), ≤43mm (males) SVL

DESCRIPTION Largest and most threatened native frog in Aotearoa/New Zealand. Dorsal surface light to dark brown, often with dark blotches, speckles and bands (particularly on hindlegs and forelimbs). Also bears conspicuous lumps (glandular ridges) on dorsolateral surfaces. Lateral surfaces often bear large black blotches. Ventral surface light brown (may be blotched). **DISTRIBUTION** Historically, found in the northwestern South Island. Now only present in Zealandia Te Māra a Tāne ecosanctuary (Te Whanganui-a-Tara/Wellington), and on several offshore islands in Raukawa Moana/Cook Strait and Marlborough Sounds. **HABITS AND HABITAT** Nocturnal (occasionally emerges on damp days). Inhabits coastal and lowland native forest and boulder banks. Forages and takes shelter among dense vegetation, leaf litter, on or under damp logs and rocks, or up trees and other plants. Does not produce a mating call. May use visual or chemical cues for reproductive behaviour. Long lived (43+ years). **CONSERVATION** Nationally Vulnerable. Has been translocated to several offshore islands and Zealandia Te Māra a Tāne ecosanctuary (Wellington), and populations are regularly monitored. The Maud Island Frog (formerly *L. pakeka*) and Hamilton's Frog were previously considered different species but have now been synonymized. However, these evolutionarily significant units are still managed separately.

Green and Golden Bell Frog ■ *Ranoidea aurea* ≤80mm (females), ≤60mm (males) SVL

DESCRIPTION Introduced to Aotearoa/New Zealand from Australia in the mid-late 1800s; large and vibrant. Dorsal surface green, brown, golden-brown, green or occasionally bright canary-yellow (in xanthochromic individuals), often with blotches and cream dorsolateral stripes. Lateral surfaces resemble dorsal surface, but typically have a very warty texture. Ventral surface pale cream-white. Bears bright blue flash markings on thighs and armpits, and conspicuous external tympana (ear drums) behind eyes. Resembles the Southern Bell Frog (opposite), but the Green and Golden Bell Frog typically has much smoother skin (v very warty) and lacks green mid-dorsal stripe (v typically present). **DISTRIBUTION** Northern New South Wales to Victoria in Australia. Widespread in Aotearoa/New Zealand from Tai Tokerau/Northland to East Cape and Taranaki (with some isolated populations in Murihiku/Southland). **HABITS AND HABITAT** Cathemeral. Inhabits ponds, slow-flowing streams, farmland, lakes and other damp vegetated areas (from the coast to subalpine areas). Forages and takes shelter in or around small bodies of water, among vegetation, on the ground, or on or under rocks and logs. Males often heard producing deep growling call. **CONSERVATION** Introduced and naturalized. Highly threatened in Australia but frequently seen in Aotearoa/New Zealand. May pose a risk for native frogs via predation and transmission of diseases (such as chytrid fungus).

Southern Bell Frog ■ *Ranoidea raniformis* ≤95mm (females), ≤65mm (males) SVL

DESCRIPTION Largest introduced frog in Aotearoa/New Zealand; colourful and warty. Dorsal surface shades of green or brown often with blotches, pale green mid-dorsal stripe and cream dorsolateral stripes. Lateral surfaces resemble dorsal surface, but typically paler with a wartier texture. Ventral surface pale cream-white. Bears bright blue flash markings on thighs and armpits, and conspicuous external tympana (ear drums) behind eyes. Skin covered with tubercles and appears very warty. Resembles the Green and Golden Bell Frog (opposite), but the Southern Bell Frog typically has wartier skin (v relatively smooth) and bears green mid-dorsal stripe (v absent).

DISTRIBUTION Only known from a few isolated populations in New South Wales, Australia. Widespread in Aotearoa/New Zealand from Tai Tokerau/Northland to Murihiku/Southland.

HABITS AND HABITAT Cathemeral. Inhabits ponds, slow-flowing streams, farmland, rocky shores, lakes and other damp vegetated areas (from the coast to alpine areas). Forages and takes shelter in or around small bodies of water, among vegetation, on the ground, or on or under rocks and logs. Males often heard producing deep growling call. **CONSERVATION** Introduced and naturalized. Highly threatened in Australia, but frequently seen in Aotearoa/New Zealand. May pose a risk for native frogs via predation and transmission of diseases (such as chytrid fungus). May comprise several unresolved species (possibly including the **Yellow-spotted Frog** *R. castanea*).

Brown (Whistling) Tree Frog ■ *Litoria ewingii* ≤49mm (females), ≤37mm (males) SVL

DESCRIPTION Introduced to Aotearoa/New Zealand from Tasmania in the late 1800s; small and robust. Dorsal surface light to dark brown, reddish-brown, cream or greenish, often with very wide brown longitudinal band, and yellow markings along dorsolateral surfaces. Lateral surfaces typically paler than dorsal surface. Ventral surface uniform cream-white. Bears bright orange flash markings on thighs, and a dark stripe that runs from each nostril through the eyes and tympana to the forelimbs. **DISTRIBUTION** Naturally widespread in southeastern Australia and Tasmania. Widespread in Aotearoa/New Zealand from Murihiku/Southland to Tai Tokerau/Northland (patchy distribution in the North Island). **HABITS AND HABITAT** Nocturnal. Inhabits range of rocky or vegetated habitats from the coast to alpine areas (often in harsh environments of more than 1,000m). Forages and takes shelter in or around small bodies of water, among vegetation, up trees, on the ground, or on or under rocks and logs. Often heard producing loud whistling call at night. Can survive being frozen. **CONSERVATION** Introduced and naturalized. May pose a risk for native frogs via transmission of diseases (such as chytrid fungus).

Green Turtle ■ *Chelonia mydas* ≤1.5m SCL

DESCRIPTION One of the largest sea turtles in the world, and perhaps the most frequently seen species in Aotearoa/New Zealand. Dorsal surfaces green, blackish, brown or yellowish. Ventral surface (plastron) pale yellowish, bluish, grey-green or white. Carapace brown, green or yellowish, with smooth non-overlapping scutes and four pairs of costal scutes. Flippers bear a single visible claw. Resembles the Hawksbill Turtle (p. 162), but the Green Turtle has a blunter snout and a single claw on each flipper (v two). Resembles the Loggerhead Turtle (p. 160), but the Green Turtle has a smaller head and one pair of prefrontal scales (v two). Resembles the Olive Ridley Turtle (p. 161), but the Green Turtle has one pair of prefrontal scales (v two), five vertebral scutes (v >five), and four pairs of costal scutes (v 5–10).

Hannah Wedig

DISTRIBUTION Widespread throughout most of the world's tropical and subtropical oceans. Found in northern Aotearoa/New Zealand (including Kermadec Islands), with few records south of Tai Tokerau/ Northland. Juveniles and subadults resident in northern Aotearoa/New Zealand. **HABITS AND HABITAT** Cathemeral. Mostly inhabits tropical and subtropical oceans. Forages in seagrass meadows, saltmarshes and reef systems. Does not breed in Aotearoa/ New Zealand. Known to live to up to 100 years. **CONSERVATION** Non-resident Native; Migrant in Aotearoa/New Zealand. Endangered throughout the world. Highly impacted by fisheries, coastal development, pollution, pathogens and climate change.

Hannah Wedig

Loggerhead Turtle ■ *Caretta caretta* ≤1.2m SCL

DESCRIPTION Second largest sea turtle in the world; rarely seen in Aotearoa/New Zealand. Dorsal surfaces cream, brown or reddish-brown. Ventral surface (plastron) pale cream or yellowish-brown. Carapace brown or reddish-brown, often with dark mottling or blotches. Flippers short and broad, with two visible claws. Refer to the Green Turtle (p. 159) and Olive Ridley Turtle (opposite) to see how the Loggerhead Turtle differs. **DISTRIBUTION** Widespread throughout the Mediterranean Sea, and Atlantic, Pacific and Indian Oceans. Found in northern Aotearoa/New Zealand, with few records south of Tai Tokerau/Northland. **HABITS AND HABITAT** Cathemeral. Inhabits tropical, subtropical and temperate oceans. Forages primarily in benthic environments, mostly on shellfish. Does not breed in Aotearoa/New Zealand. Plays an important role in recycling calcium throughout the ocean due to its shellfish consumption. **CONSERVATION** Vagrant in Aotearoa/New Zealand. Endangered throughout the world. Highly impacted by fisheries, coastal development, pollution, pathogens and climate change.

Lewis Burnett

Olive Ridley Turtle ▪ *Lepidochelys olivacea* ≤0.75m SCL

DESCRIPTION One of the smallest and most abundant sea turtles in the world; rarely seen in Aotearoa/New Zealand. Dorsal surfaces olive, greenish, greyish or grey-green. Carapace olive, greenish, greyish or grey-green. Ventral surface (plastron) off-white. Flippers bear one or two visible claws. Refer to the Green Turtle (p. 159) to see how the Olive Ridley Turtle differs. Resembles the Loggerhead Turtle (opposite), but the Olive Ridley Turtle has a proportionately smaller head and more than five vertebral scutes (v five or fewer). **DISTRIBUTION** Widespread throughout the Pacific, Indian and South Atlantic Oceans. Found throughout Aotearoa/New Zealand. **HABITS AND HABITAT** Cathemeral. Inhabits tropical and subtropical oceans. Forages mostly in shallow coastal environments. Does not breed in Aotearoa/New Zealand and is considered vagrant. Has a diverse diet comprising crustaceans, echinoderms, jellyfish, fish and algae. Known to form large breeding congregations numbering in the thousands. **CONSERVATION** Non-resident Native: Vagrant in Aotearoa/New Zealand. Vulnerable throughout the world. Impacted by fisheries, coastal development, pollution, pathogens and climate change.

Gosel Tom-Baird

Hawksbill Turtle ▪ *Eretmochelys imbricata* ≤1.1m SCL

DESCRIPTION Beautiful, distinctive and often has an ornamental, biofluorescent carapace. Dorsal surfaces dark brown, black, cream or orange-brown. Carapace brown or brown-orange, with jagged serrations along posterior margin. Often bears gorgeous contrasting dark or yellow blotches or mottling. Ventral surface (plastron) pale yellowish or white. Flippers bear two visible claws. **DISTRIBUTION** Widespread throughout tropical and subtropical waters of the Pacific, Atlantic and Indian Oceans. Found in northern

Aotearoa/New Zealand, with few records south of Tai Tokerau/Northland. **HABITS AND HABITAT** Cathemeral. Mostly inhabits tropical and subtropical oceans. Forages mainly in shallow reefs, lagoons and mangroves, on sponges, cnidarians, molluscs and crustaceans. Does not breed in Aotearoa/New Zealand. Due to the accumulation of silica, caused by the consumption of sponges, this species has toxic body tissue. **CONSERVATION** Non-resident Native: Vagrant in Aotearoa/New Zealand. Critically Endangered throughout the world. Highly impacted by fisheries, coastal development, pollution, pathogens and climate change.

Debbie Arriaga, Our Ocean Images

Debbie Arriaga, Our Ocean Images

Leatherback Turtle ■ *Dermochelys coriacea* ≤3.05m SCL

DESCRIPTION Largest sea turtle, and one of the largest reptiles on the planet. Dorsal surfaces dark grey, black or blue-black. Ventral surface (plastron) whiteish, pinkish or blue-black. Carapace dark grey, black or blue-black, with numerous pale blotches and distinctive longitudinal ridges. Flippers considerably longer (proportionately) than those of other species and lack visible claws. **DISTRIBUTION** Widespread throughout most of the world's tropical, subtropical and temperate oceans. Found throughout most of Aotearoa's/New Zealand's waters. **HABITS AND HABITAT** Cathemeral. Inhabits tropical, subtropical and temperate oceans. Forages in pelagic environments, primarily on jellyfish and salps. Does not breed in Aotearoa/New Zealand. Known to dive more than 1,000m deep and perhaps live for more than 100 years. **CONSERVATION** Non-resident Native: Migrant in Aotearoa/New Zealand. Critically Endangered throughout the world. Highly impacted by fisheries, coastal development, pollution, pathogens and climate change.

Justin Jay

Yellow-bellied Sea Snake ■ *Hydrophis platurus* ≤1.1m TL

DESCRIPTION Vibrant, highly distinctive and the most frequently observed sea snake in Aotearoa/New Zealand. Dorsal surface glossy black or yellow (rarely), with black breaking up along tail and being intercepted by bright yellow lateral colour. Ventral surface bright yellow. Head dorsoventrally flattened, and tail paddle-like and laterally flattened, with prominent black blotches. **DISTRIBUTION** The most widespread species of sea snake in the world; found throughout tropical pelagic waters of the Indian and Pacific Oceans. Occurs mostly in northern Aotearoa/New Zealand, with some records as far south as Westport in the South Island. **HABITS AND HABITAT** Diurnal, but surfaces at night to breathe. Does not reproduce in Aotearoa/New Zealand. Inhabits tropical, subtropical and temperate waters. Forages almost exclusively in pelagic environments and is fully aquatic. Known to dive more than 50m deep and remain submerged for more than three hours at a time. Bears potent neurotoxic venom but is unlikely to bite unless provoked. **CONSERVATION** Non-resident Native: Vagrant in Aotearoa/New Zealand. Least Concern throughout the world.

Will Flaxington

Yellow-lipped Sea Krait ▪ *Laticauda colubrina* ≤1.7m TL

DESCRIPTION Striking, highly venomous and the second most frequently encountered sea snake in Aotearoa/New Zealand. Dorsal surface greyish or steel-blue, with dark brown, blue or black transverse bands encircling body. Ventral surface pale grey or yellow (this colour sometimes extends on to lower lateral surfaces). Resembles Saint Giron's Sea Krait (p. 167) and the Brown-lipped Sea Krait (p. 166), but the Yellow-lipped Sea Krait has a yellow upper lip (v black or brown). **DISTRIBUTION** The most widespread species of *Laticauda*; found from eastern India to the western Pacific. Occurs in northern Aotearoa/New Zealand, with no records south of Te Whanganui-a-Tara/Wellington. **HABITS AND HABITAT** Nocturnal, but often basks on land during the day. Does not reproduce in Aotearoa/New Zealand and is rarely seen. Mostly inhabits warm tropical oceans. Forages predominantly in shallow coral reefs or mangroves. However, known to dive more than 60m deep. Known to spend much of its time on land and around rock pools. Bears potent neurotoxic venom but is shy and unlikely to bite. **CONSERVATION** Non-resident Native: Vagrant in Aotearoa/New Zealand. Least Concern throughout the world.

Daniel Solis

Brown- (Blue-) lipped Sea Krait ■ *Laticauda laticaudata* ≤1.36m TL

DESCRIPTION Beautiful, highly venomous and only recorded in Aotearoa/New Zealand once. Dorsal surface steel-blue, with dark brown, blue or black transverse bands encircling body. Ventral surface pale yellowish. Resembles the Yellow-lipped Sea Krait (p. 165) and Saint Giron's Sea Krait (opposite), but the Brown-lipped Sea Krait has a dark brown or black upper lip. **DISTRIBUTION** Widespread from eastern India to the Western Pacific. The single Aotearoa/New Zealand record occurred in Auckland. **HABITS AND HABITAT** Nocturnal, but often basks on land during the day. Does not reproduce in Aotearoa/New Zealand. Mostly inhabits warm tropical oceans. Forages predominantly in shallow coral reefs or mangroves. However, known to dive to more than 80m deep. Known to spend much of its time on land and around rock pools. Bears potent neurotoxic venom but is shy and unlikely to bite. **CONSERVATION** Non-resident Native: Vagrant in Aotearoa/New Zealand. Least Concern throughout the world.

Elsen Chen

Saint Giron's (New Caledonian) Sea Krait

■ *Laticauda saintgironsi* ≤1.6m TL

DESCRIPTION Gorgeous, highly distinctive and only recorded in Aotearoa/New Zealand once. Dorsal surface rusty brown-orange, with dark brown or black transverse bands encircling body. Ventral surface pale cream-white (this colour sometimes extends on to lower lateral surfaces). Resembles the Yellow-lipped Sea Krait (p. 165) and Brown-lipped Sea Krait (opposite), but Saint Giron's Sea Krait is a brown-orange colour (v grey or steel-blue). **DISTRIBUTION** Mostly restricted to New Caledonia and Loyalty Islands. It is not known where the single Aotearoa/New Zealand record occurred. **HABITS AND HABITAT** Nocturnal, but often basks on land during the day. Does not reproduce in Aotearoa/New Zealand. Mostly inhabits tropical and subtropical waters. Forages predominantly in shallow coastal waters. However, known to dive to more than 80m deep. Known to spend much of its time on land and climb trees, and has been recorded at more than 100m elevation. Bears potent neurotoxic venom but is shy and unlikely to bite. **CONSERVATION** Non-resident Native: Vagrant in Aotearoa/New Zealand. Least Concern throughout the world.

Lennart Hudel

■ Checklist of Reptiles & Amphibians ■

This comprehensive checklist features every reptile and amphibian taxon that occurs in Aotearoa/New Zealand.

Most of the country's herpetofauna do not have a global IUCN threat status. For consistency, the Aotearoa/New Zealand conservation statuses for all species have been used. These are based on Hitchmough, 2021, 'Conservation status of New Zealand reptiles' (see bibliography, p. 172). Geckos have been grouped in their respective genera, and skinks in the major island they belong to (in some cases they occupy both islands, so two species are listed twice), and the remaining reptiles and amphibians in their respective genera, families or superfamilies. Note that the species descriptions provide the relevant Aotearoa/New Zealand Conservation status for each taxon. However, for simplicity, the categories (for example At Risk) have been removed in the descriptions.

Categories & Abbreviations

AR	At Risk	**NRN**	Non-resident Native
D	Declining	**NT**	Not Threatened
DD	Data Deficient	**NU**	Naturally Uncommon
IN	Introduced & Naturalized	**NV**	Nationally Vulnerable
M	Migrant	**R**	Relict
NC	Nationally Critical	**RC**	Recovering
NE	Nationally Endangered	**T**	Threatened
NI	Nationally Increasing	**V**	Vagrant

Common Name	Scientific Name	Category	Conservation Status
Sphenodontidae (Tuatara)			
Tuatara	*Sphenodon punctatus*	AR	R
Diplodactylidae (Geckos)			
Tukutuku			
Harlequin Gecko	*Tukutuku rakiurae*	T	NE
Naultinus (Green Geckos)			
Aupōuri Gecko	*Naultinus flavirictus*	AR	D
Northland Green Gecko	*Naultinus grayii*	AR	D
Elegant Gecko	*Naultinus elegans*	AR	D
Barking Gecko	*Naultinus punctatus*	AR	D
Marlborough Green Gecko	*Naultinus manukanus*	AR	D
Rough Gecko	*Naultinus rudis*	T	NE
Starred Gecko	*Naultinus stellatus*	T	NV
West Coast Green Gecko	*Naultinus tuberculatus*	T	NV
Jewelled Gecko	*Naultinus gemmeus*	AR	D
Toropuku (Striped Geckos)			
Northern Striped Gecko	*Toropuku inexpectatus*	T	NV
Southern Striped Gecko	*Toropuku stephensi*	T	NV
Mokopirirakau (Forest Geckos)			
Ngahere Gecko	*Mokopirirakau* 'Southern North Island'	AR	D
Forest Gecko	*Mokopirirakau granulatus*	AR	D
Black-eyed Gecko	*Mokopirirakau kahutarae*	T	NV
Hura te ao Gecko	*Mokopirirakau galaxias*	T	NE

Common Name	Scientific Name	Category	Conservation Status
Broad-cheeked Gecko	Mokopirirakau 'Ōkārito'	T	NV
Open Bay Islands Gecko	Mokopirirakau 'Open Bay Islands'	T	NE
Cascades Gecko	Mokopirirakau 'Cascades'	AR	D
Orange-spotted Gecko	Mokopirirakau 'Roys Peak'	AR	D
Tautuku Gecko	Mokopiriakau 'Southern Forest'	AR	D
Tākitimu Gecko	Mokopirirakau cryptozoicus	T	NV
Cloudy Gecko	Mokopirirakau nebulosus	AR	R
Dactylocnemis (Pacific Geckos)			
Pacific Gecko	Dactylocnemis pacificus	NT	NT
Matapia Gecko	Dactylocnemis 'Matapia Island'	AR	D
Te Paki Gecko	Dactylocnemis 'North Cape'	AR	D
Three Kings Gecko	Dactylocnemis 'Three Kings'	AR	NU
Poor Knights Gecko	Dactylocnemis 'Poor Knights'	AR	NU
Mokohinau Gecko	Dactylocnemis 'Mokohinau'	AR	NU
Hoplodactylus (Duvaucel's Geckos)			
Northern Duvaucel's Gecko	Hoplodactylus duvauceli	AR	R
Southern Duvaucel's Gecko	Hoplodactylus duvauceli 'Southern'	T	NI
Woodworthia (Rock Geckos)			
Raukawa Gecko	Woodworthia maculata	NT	NT
Muriwai Gecko	Woodworthia aff. maculata 'Muriwai'	T	NV
Goldstripe Gecko	Woodworthia chrysosiretica	AR	D
Kahurangi Gecko	Woodworthia 'Mount Arthur'	AR	D
Sabine Gecko	Woodworthia 'Sabine'	DD	DD
Minimac Gecko	Woodworthia 'Marlborough Mini'	AR	D
Kaikouras Gecko	Woodworthia 'Kaikouras'	AR	D
Pygmy Gecko	Woodworthia 'Pygmy'	AR	D
Waitaha Gecko	Woodworthia cf. brunnea	AR	D
Greywacke Gecko	Woodworthia 'Southern Alps Northern'	AR	D
Southern Alps Gecko	Woodworthia 'Southern Alps'	AR	D
Raggedy Range Gecko	Woodworthia 'Raggedy Range'	T	NV
Schist Gecko	Woodworthia 'Central Otago'	AR	D
Kawarau Gecko	Woodworthia 'Cromwell'	AR	D
Kōrero Gecko	Woodworthia 'Otago/Southland Large'	AR	D
Mountain Beech Gecko	Woodworthia 'Southwestern Large'	AR	D
Short-toed Gecko	Woodworthia 'Southern mini'	AR	D
Scincidae (Introduced Skinks)			
Delicate (Rainbow) Skink	Lampropholis delicata	IN	IN
Scincidae (Native Skinks)			
Oligosoma (North Island Skinks)			
Copper Skink	Oligosoma aeneum	AR	D
Slight Skink	Oligosoma levidensum	T	NE
Hardy's Skink	Oligosoma hardyi	AR	NU
Aorangi Skink	Oligosoma roimata	AR	NU
Ornate Skink	Oligosoma ornatum	AR	D
Hauraki Skink	Oligosoma townsi	AR	RC
Coromandel Skink	Oligosoma pachysomaticum	AR	R
Marbled Skink	Oligosoma oliveri	AR	NU
Whitaker's Skink	Oligosoma whitakeri	T	NE
McGregor's Skink	Oligosoma mcgregori	AR	RC

■ CHECKLIST ■

Common Name	Scientific Name	Category	Conservation Status
Robust Skink	*Oligosoma alani*	AR	RC
Falla's Skink	*Oligosoma fallai*	AR	NU
Chevron Skink	*Oligosoma homalonotum*	T	NV
Striped Skink	*Oligosoma striatum*	AR	D
Glossy Brown Skink	*Oligosoma zelandicum*	AR	D
Kakerakau Skink	*Oligosoma kakerakau*	T	NC
Moko Skink	*Oligosoma moco*	AR	R
Egg-laying Skink	*Oligosoma suteri*	AR	R
Shore Skink	*Oligosoma smithi*	AR	D
Tātahi Skink	*Oligosoma aff. smithi* 'Three Kings, Te Paki, Western Northland'	AR	D
Small-scaled Skink	*Oligosoma microlepis*	T	NV
Crenulate Skink	*Oligosoma robinsoni*	AR	D
Hawke's Bay Skink	*Oligosoma auroraense*	T	NE
Kupe Skink	*Oligosoma aff. infrapunctatum* 'Southern North Island'	T	NC
Northern Grass Skink	*Oligosoma polychroma*	NT	NT
Northern Spotted Skink	*Oligosoma kokowai*	AR	R
Oligosoma (South Island Skinks)			
Newman's Speckled Skink	*Oligosoma newmani*	AR	D
Cobble Skink	*Oligosoma aff. infrapunctatum* 'Cobble'	T	NC
Alborn Skink	*Oligosoma albornense*	T	NC
Kapitia Skink	*Oligosoma salmo*	T	NC
Hokitika Skink	*Oligosoma aff. infrapunctatum* 'Hokitika'	T	NC
Boulenger's Speckled Skink	*Oligosoma infrapunctatum*	DD	DD
Westport Skink	*Oligosoma aff. infrapunctatum* 'Westport'	DD	DD
Ōkārito Skink	*Oligosoma aff. infrapunctatum* 'Ōkārito'	DD	DD
Chathams Skink	*Oligosoma nigriplantare*	AR	R
Northern Grass Skink	*Oligosoma polychroma*	NT	NT
Waiharakeke Grass Skink	*Oligosoma aff. polychroma* Clade 2	AR	D
South Marlborough Grass Skink	*Oligosoma aff. polychroma* Clade 3	AR	D
Canterbury Grass Skink	*Oligosoma aff. polychroma* Clade 4	AR	D
Southern Grass Skink	*Oligosoma aff. polychroma* Clade 5	AR	D
McCann's Skink	*Oligosoma maccani*	NT	NT
Nevis Skink	*Oligosoma toka*	AR	D
Burgan Skink	*Oligosoma burganae*	T	NE
Eyres Skink	*Oligosoma repens*	AR	D
Mataura Skink	*Oligosoma* 'Mataura Range'	DD	DD
Rockhopper Skink	*Oligosoma* 'Rockhopper'	AR	D
Big Bay Skink	*Oligosoma aff. inconspicuum* 'Big Bay'	T	NV
Mahogany Skink	*Oligosoma aff. inconspicuum* 'Mahogany'	AR	D
Oteake Skink	*Oligosoma aff. inconspicuum* 'Oteake'	T	NV
Pallid Skink	*Oligosoma aff. inconspicuum* 'Pallid'	AR	D
Herbfield Skink	*Oligosoma aff. inconspicuum* 'Herbfield'	AR	D
Cryptic Skink	*Oligosoma inconspicuum*	AR	D
Te Kākahu Skink	*Oligosoma tekakahu*	T	NE
Southern Skink	*Oligosoma notosaurus*	AR	D
Small-eared Skink	*Oligosoma stenotis*	T	NV
Okuru Skink	*Oligosoma* 'Okuru'	DD	DD

Common Name	Scientific Name	Category	Conservation Status
Kahurangi Skink	*Oligosoma kahurangi*	T	NC
Long-toed Skink	*Oligosoma longipes*	T	NV
Roamatimati Skink	*Oligosoma* aff. *longipes* 'Southern'	AR	D
White-bellied Skink	*Oligosoma hoparatea*	T	NC
Northern Spotted Skink	*Oligosoma kokowai*	AR	R
Marlborough Spotted Skink	*Oligosoma elium*	T	NE
Canterbury Spotted Skink	*Oligosoma lineoocellatum*	T	NV
Mackenzie Skink	*Oligosoma prasinum*	T	NV
Lakes Skink	*Oligosoma* aff. *chloronoton* 'West Otago'	T	NV
Otago Green Skink	*Oligosoma* aff. *chloronoton* 'Eastern Otago'	AR	D
Southland Green Skink	*Oligosoma chloronoton*	T	NE
Stewart Island Green Skink	*Oligosoma* aff. *chloronoton* 'Stewart Island'	T	NV
Grand Skink	*Oligosoma grande*	T	NE
Otago Skink	*Oligosoma otagense*	T	NE
Marlborough Scree Skink	*Oligosoma* aff. *waimatense* 'Marlborough'	T	NE
Scree Skink	*Oligosoma waimatense*	T	NV
Alpine Rock Skink	*Oligosoma* aff. *waimatense* 'Alpine Rock'	T	NV
Taumaka Skink	*Oligosoma taumakae*	T	NE
Fiordland Skink	*Oligosoma acrinasum*	T	NV
Awakopaka Skink	*Oligosoma awakopaka*	T	NC
Barrier Skink	*Oligosoma judgei*	T	NE
Sinbad Skink	*Oligosoma pikitanga*	T	NE
Leiopelmatidae (Native Frogs)			
Hochstetter's Frog	*Leiopelma hochstetteri*	AR	D
Archey's Frog	*Leiopelma archeyi*	AR	D
Hamilton's Frog	*Leiopelma hamiltoni*	T	NV
Pelodryadidae (Introduced Frogs)			
Green and Golden Bell Frog	*Ranoidea aurea*	IN	IN
Southern Bell Frog	*Ranoidea raniformis*	IN	IN
Brown (Whistling) Tree Frog	*Litoria ewingii*	IN	IN
Chelonioidea (Marine Turtles)			
Cheloniidae			
Green Turtle	*Chelonia mydas*	NRN	M
Loggerhead Turtle	*Caretta caretta*	NRN	V
Olive Ridley Turtle	*Lepidochelys olivacea*	NRN	V
Hawksbill Turtle	*Eretmochelys imbricata*	NRN	V
Dermochelyidae			
Leatherback Turtle	*Dermochelys coriacea*	NRN	M
Elapidae (Marine Snakes)			
Hydrophiinae			
Yellow-bellied Sea Snake	*Hydrophis platurus*	NRN	V
Laticaudinae			
Yellow-lipped Sea Krait	*Laticauda colubrina*	NRN	V
Brown- Blue-) lipped Sea Krait	*Laticauda laticaudata*	NRN	V
Saint Giron's Sea Krait	*Laticauda saintgironsi*	NRN	V

Bibliography

Barr, B. P., Chapple, D. G., Hitchmough, R. A., Patterson, G. B. & Board, N. T. 2021. A new species of *Oligosoma* (Squamata: Scincidae) from the northern North Island, New Zealand. *Zootaxa*, 5047(4), 401–415.

Bell, T. P. & Patterson, G. B. 2008. A rare alpine skink *Oligosoma pikitanga* n. sp. (Reptilia: Scincidae) from Llawrenny Peaks, Fiordland, New Zealand. *Zootaxa*, 1882(1), 57–68.

Bertoia, A., Monks, J., Knox, C. & Cree, A. 2021. A nocturnally foraging gecko of the high-latitude alpine zone: Extreme tolerance of cold nights, with cryptic basking by day. *Journal of Thermal Biology*, 99, 102957.

Carey Knox. 2021. Flickr page. https://www.flickr.com/photos/151723530@N05/albums.

Daugherty, C. H., Maxson, L. R. & Bell, B. D. 1982. Phylogenetic relationships within the New Zealand frog genus *Leiopelma* – immunological evidence. *New Zealand Journal of Zoology*, 9(2), 239–242.

Easton, L. 2018. *Taxonomy and genetic management of New Zealand's Leiopelma frogs* (Doctoral dissertation, University of Otago).

Hitchmough, R. A., Nielsen, S. V., Lysaght, J. A. & Bauer, A. M. 2021. A new species of *Naultinus* from the Te Paki area, northern New Zealand. *Zootaxa*, 4915(3), zootaxa-4915.

Hitchmough, R. A., Barr, B., Knox, C., Lettink, M., Monks, J. M., Patterson, G. B., Reardon, J. T., van Winkel, D., Rolfe, J. & Michel, P. 2021. Conservation status of New Zealand reptiles, 2021. *New Zealand Threat Classification Series 35*. Department of Conservation, Te Whanganui-a-Tara/Wellington.

Hugall, A. F., Foster, R. & Lee, M. S. 2007. Calibration choice, rate smoothing, and the pattern of tetrapod diversification according to the long nuclear gene RAG-1. *Systematic Biology*, 56(4), 543–563.

Jewell, T. 2008. *A Photographic Guide to Reptiles and Amphibians of New Zealand*. New Holland.

Jewell, T. 2019. *Southern skinks of New Zealand – a field guide, edition four*. Jewell Publications. PDF download at: www.facebook.com/groups/1762900770661188.

Jewell, T. R. 2019. New Zealand forest-dwelling skinks of the *Oligosoma oliveri* (McCann) species-complex (Reptilia: Scincidae): reinstatement of *O. pachysomaticum* (Robb) and an assessment of historical distribution ranges. *Zootaxa*, 4688(3), zootaxa-4688.

Jewell, T. R., & Leschen, R. A. (2004). A new species of *Hoplodactylus* (Reptilia: Pygopodidae) from the Takitimu Mountains, South Island, New Zealand. *Zootaxa*, 792(1), 1–11.

Jewell, Tony. 2021. Flickr page. www.flickr.com/photos/rocknvole/albums.

Knox, C., Hitchmough, R. A., Nielsen, S. V., Jewell, T. & Bell, T. 2021. A new, enigmatic species of black-eyed gecko (Reptilia: Diplodactylidae: *Mokopirirakau*) from North Otago, New Zealand. *Zootaxa*, 4964(1), zootaxa-4964.

Melzer, S., Bell, T. & Patterson, G. B. 2017. Hidden conservation vulnerability within a cryptic species complex: taxonomic revision of the spotted skink (*Oligosoma lineoocellatum*; Reptilia: Scincidae) from New Zealand. *Zootaxa*, 4300(3), 355–379.

Melzer, S., Hitchmough, R. A., Bell, T., Chapple, D. G. & Patterson, G. B. 2019. Lost and found: taxonomic revision of the speckled skink (*Oligosoma infrapunctatum*; Reptilia; Scincidae) species complex from New Zealand reveals a potential cryptic extinction, resurrection of two species, and description of three new species. *Zootaxa*, 4623(3), zootaxa-4623.

New Zealand Herpetological Society. 2021. *Herpetofauna index*. www.reptiles.org.nz/herpetofauna-index.

Nielsen, S. V., Bauer, A. M., Jackman, T. R., Hitchmough, R. A. & Daugherty, C. H. 2011. New Zealand geckos (Diplodactylidae): cryptic diversity in a post-Gondwanan lineage with trans-Tasman affinities. *Molecular Phylogenetics and Evolution*, 59(1), 1–22.

Patterson, G. B. & Bell, T. P. 2009. The Barrier skink *Oligosoma judgei* n. sp. (Reptilia: Scincidae) from the Darran and Takitimu Mountains, South Island, New Zealand. *Zootaxa*, 2271(1), 43–56.

Patterson, G. B. & Hitchmough, R. A. 2021. A new alpine skink species (Scincidae: Eugongylinae: *Oligosoma*) from Kahurangi National Park, New Zealand. *Zootaxa*, 4920(4), zootaxa-4920.

Scarsbrook, L. 2021. *Does size matter? using osteology and ancient DNA to reconstruct extinct diversity in Duvaucel's Gecko* (Doctoral dissertation, University of Otago).

Tocher, M. D. 2003. The diet of grand skinks (*Oligosoma grande*) and Otago skinks (*O. otagense*) in Otago seral tussock grasslands. *New Zealand Journal of Zoology*, 30(3), 243–257.

van Winkel, D., Baling, M. & Hitchmough, R. 2020. *Reptiles and Amphibians of New Zealand*. Bloomsbury Publishing.

Wallis, G. P. & Jorge, F. 2018. Going under down under? Lineage ages argue for extensive survival of the Oligocene marine transgression on Zealandia. *Molecular Ecology*, 27(22), 4368–4396.

Whitaker, T., Chapple, D. G., Hitchmough, R. A., Lettink, M. & Patterson, G. B. 2018. A new species of scincid lizard in the genus *Oligosoma* (Reptilia: Scincidae) from the mid-Canterbury high country, New Zealand. *Zootaxa*, 4377(2), 269–279.

Submission of Records

To fill out and submit an Amphibian and Reptile Distribution Scheme (ARDS) card to the Department of Conservation, contact www.doc.govt.nz/our-work/reptiles-and-frogs-distribution/atlas/species-sightings-and-data-management/report-a-sighting. These records are stored in a database that is incredibly useful for informing conservation and management decisions

The following website enables you to seek identification assistance for most observations. However, please ensure the specific location of any herpetofauna found is obscured, and only a general location is provided: https://inaturalist.nz/ (iNaturalist NZ).

This Facebook group also enables you to seek identification assistance for most observations. However, please ensure that the specific location of any herpetofauna found is obscured, and only a general location is provided. www.facebook.com/groups/228066221073092 (NZ Lizard identification expert – expert ID).

Acknowledgements

There are many people who have supported me with my herpetological endeavours that I would like to thank expressly. Several of these inspiring people have meticulously proofread my writing and provided me with invaluable information that was critical for producing this book. Many others have generously donated photographs or allowed me to photograph captive native reptiles they care for. Finally, some have cared for me, cared for my invertebrates while I have been in the field or simply facilitated my passion for wildlife in a meaningful way. I cannot express my gratitude enough to these people. Thank you to Hannah Wedig, Sara Purdie, Mark Purdie, Elizabeth Purdie, the Marwick family, Karen and Gary Davis, Keegan Pepper, Mikaere Berryman-Kamp, James Liu, Eric Leung, Ihaia Anderson, Daichi Ito, Oscar Thomas, John Beaufoy, Rosemary Wilkinson, Krystyna Mayer, Carey Knox, Tony Jewell, Nick Harker, Tim Harker, Phil Bishop, Debbie Bishop, Jo Monks, Karina Sidaway, Trent Bell, Cameron Thorpe, Lynn Adams, Les Moran, Marieke Lettink, Tom Gunn, Ben Barr, James Reardon, Dylan van Winkel, Mandy Tocher, Rod Hitchmough, Luke Easton, Murray Efford, Petrina Duncan, Sara Smerdon, Rogier Goessens, Mahakirau Forest Estate, Emily Edkins, Dave Laux, Ben Goodwin, Auckland Zoo, Taylor Davies-Colley, Madeleine Post, Alex McKevitt, Clare Gunton, Katie Gray, Jade Christiansen, Joel Knight, Dennis Keall, Reino Grundling, Euan Brooke, Phil Melgren, Ben Weatherly, Elson Chen, Massimiliano Finzi, Justin Jay, Debbie and Jerry Arriaga, Lewis Burnett, Pierre-Louis Stenger, Lennart Hudel, Gosel Tom-Baird, Will Flaxington, Susan Newall, Shaun Murphy, Michelle Knox, Mark Paterson, Colin Miskelly, The Museum of New Zealand Te Papa Tongarewa, Jean-Claude Stahl, Craig Stonyer, Rheanne Sullivan and all of the marvellous reptiles and amphibians that I have been fortunate enough to photograph.

▪ INDEX ▪